52
GREAT POKER
TIPS

52 GREAT POKER TIPS

Lou Krieger

BATSFORD

First published in the United Kingdom in 2007 by
Batsford
151 Freston Road
London W10 6TH

An imprint of Anova Books Company Ltd

ISBN–13 9780713490350

A CIP catalogue record for this book is available from the British Library.

15 14 13 12 11 10 09 08 07
10 9 8 7 6 5 4 3 2 1

Reproduction by Classicscan, Singapore
Printed and bound by MPG Books Ltd, Bodmin, Cornwall

This book can be ordered direct from the publisher at the website:
www.anovabooks.com, or try your local bookshop

Distributed in the United States and Canada by Sterling Publishing Co.,
387 Park Avenue South, New York, NY 10016, USA

This book is dedicated to my wife, Deirdre Quinn. The odds against love are longer than those of any poker hand, but some people are fortunate enough to be lucky in love and poker too. Thanks to her, I'm one of them.

Lou Krieger

Contents

Introduction

There's never been a better time to learn poker. With the advent of the lipstick camera – a tiny camera pioneered by the World Poker Tour that is positioned next to each competitor and shows the television audience what the players can't see: each other's cards – poker has become a spectator sport and its popularity has sent TV ratings through the roof. More and more people are learning how to play for the first time, or brushing up on their game if all they've ever done before is learn the rudiments in order to play at the kitchen table with family and friends.

Although the players you see on television and those entering high buy-in tournaments such as the World Poker Tour and the World Series of Poker are incredibly skilled, most of the new players coming into the game are not. The majority of poker players you'll encounter have never read a poker book in their lives.

Just a bit of study will give you an edge over most of the players you'll encounter in casino poker games. You can even earn money-playing poker without having to be a world-class player. All you have to do is be able to beat your opponents. You can't say that about most other sports and games. If you're not one of the top tennis players in the world, or one of the best basketball players, or a world-class golfer, you might enjoy the sport as a hobby, but you can't count on it to supplement your income.

But when you're playing poker, you needn't be as skilful as a World Series of Poker winner to make a buck from your favourite hobby or avocation. You just have to keep one step ahead of your opponents. It's all relative, and a little learning gives you a big edge.

This surge of interest in poker has resulted in a publishing bonanza for poker books aimed at players at all levels of skill and development. This book is aimed at beginning poker players as well as more experienced players, who might have a lot of table time under their belt, but who have not taken the time to study the game. I know about most of these books. I've written ten of them myself.

The format of *52 Great Poker Tips* is straightforward. Following an introduction to Texas hold'em poker there are 52 tips – one for each card in the deck. If you learn the game and learn these tips, you will profit from them. Just applying one tip each time you visit a card room or casino can produce money in your pocket or save you from the devastation of a really bad day at the tables.

You are living during hold'em's good old days. That's right. There's never been a better time to learn the game, or a better time to ply your skill at the tables. With all the newbies flocking to casinos and cardrooms everywhere – including cybercasinos that can be accessed from the Internet – games are typically filled with beginning players who are less skilled than you. At lower betting limit games, you might find an entire table filled with beginners.

It's a gold rush for good players. So pick up this book, read the tips and improve your game. Although this book is aimed at beginning players, the truths in these tips can be applied to all games, even those filled with skilful players.

While this book shouldn't be your complete poker education – no single book can hope to accomplish that – it's a beginning aimed at grounding you in proper play and allowing you to spread your wings and grow as a player.

If You've Never Played Texas Hold'em Before

Poker is a collection of games with common attributes such as hand rankings, betting and bluffing. In Texas hold'em, the highest poker hand wins. Other forms of poker reward the lowest hand, and in still others the highest and lowest hands split the pot.

Poker differs from the vast majority of casino games because it's you against the house in casino games, and the odds are always in the house's favour. Poker players don't compete against the house; they're just trying to beat the other players. The house is your host and makes its money by raking a token sum from each pot, or collecting a time charge from each player every 30 minutes, to pay for the table, chips, chairs and a trained, professional dealer.

Poker is a game of money that's played with cards. Underlying each strategy in poker is the relationship between the odds against making your hand and the size of the pot. It is a constantly changing environment where choices are usually made on incomplete information. Although luck is significant in the short run, players making better decisions than their opponents are certain to be rewarded over the long haul.

That's another way of saying that your decisions matter in poker. In the long run, whether you decide to choose black or red at the roulette table doesn't matter at all. But decision-making matters at poker, and at the end of the day the best decisions usually determine the winners.

Poker players exercise control over their actions. Can I make better decisions than my opponents? If I can, I will be rewarded – with matchsticks or millions – depending on my willingness to take a risk and back it with logic, knowledge of my opponents and my instincts. A little luck never hurts, either.

Texas hold'em, which is far and away the most popular form of poker, is a simple game to learn. The objective is to win money. You accomplish this by winning *pots* – the money or chips wagered during the play of each hand.

A pot can be won by showing down (revealing) the best hand at the conclusion of the betting rounds. When two or more players are still active after all the betting rounds are completed, they turn their hands face up. The pot then goes to the player holding the best hand.

Pots are also won when all players but one have folded, thereby relinquishing their interest in the pot. The winner may have the best hand or may have been *bluffing* – it doesn't matter. When everyone else surrenders their claim to the pot, it belongs to the last man – or woman – standing.

Hand Rankings
Poker is played with a standard 52-card deck comprised of four suits: spades, hearts, diamonds and clubs. Each suit is equal in value and there are thirteen cards of each suit. An ace is the highest-ranking card in a suit, followed by king, queen, jack and ten down to two (or deuce) in descending order. An ace may also be used as the lowest ranking card in a five-high straight (5-4-3-2-A), which is also called a *wheel* or *bicycle*.

Although Texas hold'em is played with seven cards, the best hand refers to the best five-card hand. Hand rankings are a function of probability: the rarer the hand, the more valuable it is.

Straight flush
A straight flush is five cards of the same suit in sequence, such as 9♥8♥7♥6♥5♥. A royal flush is simply an ace-high straight flush – A♠K♠Q♠J♠10♠ – and is the best possible hand in poker.

Four-of-a-kind

Four-of-a-kind, or 'quads,' is a five-card hand comprised of all the cards of one rank plus one unrelated card, such as J♥J♠J♦J♣5♣. The higher the rank, the better the hand.

Full house

Three cards of one rank and a pair of another make a full house. The rank of the full house is determined by the three-card grouping, not the pair. A hand like 9♥9♠9♦5♦5♣ is referred to as nines full of fives and would beat a lower full house such as 8♠8♥8♣A♣A♥.

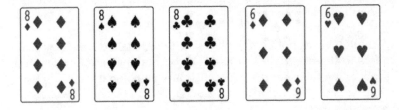

Flush

A flush is any five cards of the same suit, in any sequence. If there is more than one flush, the winning hand is determined by the rank order of the highest card – or cards – in the flush. A flush comprised of A♥Q♥J♥6♥5♥ is higher than A♥Q♥J♥4♥3♥.

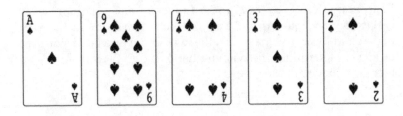

Straight

A straight is five cards in sequence but not all the same suit. If more than one straight is present, the highest card in the sequence determines the winning hand. For example, J♥T♠9♦8♦7♣ (jack-high straight) beats 9♠8♠7♦6♠5♣ (nine-high straight).

Three-of-a-kind

Three cards of the same rank plus two unrelated cards makes a hand called three-of-a-kind. Poker players refer to three-of-a-kind as trips or a set. If you held 8♣8♥8♠K♦4♣ you could refer to it as trip eights or a set of eights.

Two pair

Two cards of identical rank along with two cards of a different but identical rank, plus one unrelated card, comprise two pair. When more than one player has two pair, the highest ranked pair determines which hand is superior. If two players have the same higher pair, then the rank of the lower pair determines the winner. For example, Q♣Q♥8♠8♦4♣ (queens and eights) beats Q♠Q♦5♣5♠K♦ (queens and fives). If both players hold the same higher and lower two pair, then the rank of the unrelated side card, or kicker, determines the winning hand. If two players' hands are identical, they split the pot.

One pair

One pair is simply two cards of one rank plus three unrelated cards. If two players hold the same pair, then the highest unrelated side card determines the winning hand.

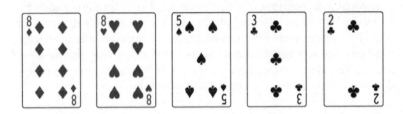

No pair or high card

Five unrelated cards. When no player has at least a pair, the winning hand is determined by the rank order of the unrelated cards. For example, if only one hand contains an ace, that hand is the winner. If two hands contain an ace, the second-highest card determines the winner, and so on.

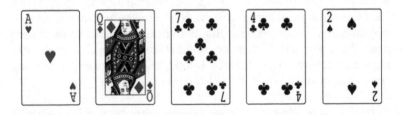

Betting

Betting is poker's key element. Minimizing losses when holding a poor hand while maximizing wins with good hands by betting or saving bets is what poker is all about.

Texas hold'em has four betting rounds. In the first round, each player in turn must decide whether to call (match the bet), raise the blind bet or any prior raises, or else fold. The second, third and fourth rounds require a check or a bet from the player who is first to act, and then each player in clockwise rotation may either check or bet if no preceding player has bet. Once a bet has been made, players must choose to either fold, call or raise.

When a player folds, he relinquishes all claim to the hand along with any chips he may have contributed to the pot. After the last round of wagering, a showdown among active players, when the hands are revealed, determines the winner.

How much can you bet?

In a *fixed-limit* game, no one may bet or raise more than a predetermined number of chips. This limit usually varies with the round of the game. Betting limits double on the third wagering round in most Texas hold'em formats. If you were playing Texas hold'em and the betting limits were $10–$20, during the first two rounds bets would be in increments of $10. Those increments would double to $20 on the last two rounds of wagering.

Spread-limit games allow bettors to wager any amount within the limits. A limit might be $2–$10, which means that any wager between $2 and $10 is permitted, with the proviso that a raise must be at least the equal of the bet that preceded it.

In most limit games, a bet and either three or four raises per betting round are permitted.

In *pot-limit*, bets or raises are limited only by the amount of money in the pot when the wager is made. A player who raises may count his call as part of the pot. If there is $10 in the pot, and someone wagers $10, a raiser may call that bet, making the pot $30 and then raise the entire pot. When he is done, the pot will contain $60. However, always state that you intend to raise before placing any chips into the pot.

In *no-limit*, a player may bet or raise any amount of chips he has in front of him at any time.

Table stakes

You can't add chips or money to the amount you have on the table during the play of a hand. If you run out of money, you can only compete for the portion of the pot that your bets cover. Casino games in the USA and most European countries are always table stakes. However, if you are in an unfamiliar place for the first time, always ask about the local rules.

Going all-in

If you cannot cover a bet or raise, or if you are playing no-limit and wish to commit all your chips to the pot, you are said to be *all-in*. An all-in player can only vie for the portion of the pot his or her money covers. Other active players may still wager into a *side pot*. At the hand's conclusion, the winner of the side pot is decided first, then the winner of the main pot.

Only the players who bet into the side pot are eligible to win it, but everyone who played the hand to its conclusion or went all-in is eligible for the main pot. It's possible to have more than one side pot if more than one player goes all-in at different points in the hand, and it's possible to have more than one winner at the showdown. An all-in player, or any other player for that matter, can always purchase more chips between hands.

String-raises are forbidden

Calling a bet and then reaching back for more chips and announcing a raise is called a *string raise* and is not allowed. This rule prevents a player from reading the reactions of his opponents while he puts some chips in the pot and then deciding to raise if he thinks he's got the best of it.

Protect your hand

A poker player, like a boxer, should protect himself at all times. If you aren't certain whether yours is the best hand at the showdown, turn it face up and let the dealer make that determination. Although in most places cards speak, dealers can make mistakes. If you believe you hold the winning hand, turn your cards face up and announce it. There's no penalty if you're wrong and it may get you the pot if the dealer misread your hand and you're right.

Blind bets and dealer button

Every poker hand begins with *blind* bets, mandatory bets made by the two players to the left of the *dealer button*, a white disk designating the player who would be the dealer if the game did not have a professional dealer.

The purpose of a blind bet – usually called a *blind* – is to tempt and tantalize players, enticing them into the pot and creating action because there's some money to win.

Basic poker strategy

Without a basis for making decisions about whether to call, fold, raise or re-raise, poker is a lottery. But, played properly, it's a game of skill. Each pot contains money, and winning money is what's important. Winning pots is only incidental. Winning money means tempering enthusiasm with realism by being selective about the hands you play.

To win the most pots, all you'd have to do is play every hand, call every bet, and you'd win every pot you possibly could. But you'd lose money in the process. Skilled players engage in few hands, but they look for ways to maximize the amount they win when the odds seem to favour them.

This is really what poker is all about. Anyone can win in the short run. But over the long haul – when the cards have evened out – the better players will win more money with their good hands and lose less money with weak hands than will their adversaries.

How to play Texas hold'em

Texas hold'em uses blind bets that are posted by the two players to the left of the rotating dealer button. In a game with betting increments of two and four dollars, the blinds will be one and two dollars.

Two cards are dealt face down to each player, followed by a round of betting. Each player, beginning with the player to the left of the two-dollar blind, may fold, call that two-dollar bet, or raise. The player who posted the one-dollar blind bet has an option to fold, call or raise, and the player who posted the two-dollar blind may also raise his own blind bet. In fixed-limit games, a bet and either three or four raises per betting round are permitted.

If two or more players are active when the first betting round ends, three cards, called the *flop*, are turned up in the centre of the table. These cards may be used by each player in combination with his or her own two cards. Another round of betting follows. A fourth communal card, called the *turn*, is dealt and there's another round of betting, this time in four-dollar increments.

If at least two players are still vying for the pot, a fifth and final communal card, called the *river*, is turned up and the last wagering round takes place. If two or more players remain at the conclusion of all the betting rounds, a showdown determines the best hand.

Six Quick Tips for Winning Hold'em Play

If you play hold'em correctly, you'll have incorporated all of these tips into your game.

✓ Play few hands from early position. You'll throw lots of hands away, but you'll be saving money.

✓ Position is critical in hold'em. Be aware that hands that you would fold in an early position can be raising hands in late position.

✓ Fit or fold: If the flop does not help your hand, you must consider folding, regardless of how sweet it may have looked before the flop.

✓ Tread carefully. Many of your opponents will play A-K as strongly as a pair of aces or kings, but it is not. A-K is a powerful drawing hand but it usually needs help on the flop to win the pot.

✓ Note that the use of community cards, the positional aspect of the game, and the fact that on the flop you will see 71 per cent of your hand for the cost of a single round of betting, means the best hand on the flop stands a good chance of holding up.

✓ Be selective and aggressive – these are the keys to success.

Tip 1   Better Betting

Betting is what poker is all about. We usually bet when we have the best hand and whenever we think a well-timed bluff will win the pot without murmur or protest from an adversary across the table, even if he or she has a slightly better hand right now.

Those pulse-raising moments when you drag a large pot feel terrific. But they don't happen as often as you'd like. If you raised with A-K before the flop, you'll flop a pair of aces or kings only about one-third of the time. Most of the time the flop won't improve your hand and you'll be left to decide what to do about it.

Sometimes decisions are easy. Against three or more opponents you're usually safe in assuming that at least one of your opponents likes the flop, and if the flop was no help to your hand, you're probably an underdog right now.

If someone bets, you can fold, forget about that once promising A-K and get ready for the next hand.

But it's different if your ace and king are suited and two cards of your suit appear on the flop. Now you have a draw to the best possible flush and any one of the nine remaining unseen cards of your suit will complete your hand. If an ace or a king comes on the turn you also stand a good chance of winning. After all, top pair with the very best side card, or *kicker*, wins a lot of hold'em confrontations.

If the board (the community cards on the table) does not contain a pair – and a board without a pair cannot provide a full house or four-of-a-kind to an opponent – any of those nine flush cards will turn your hand into a sure winner and any of the other three aces or tree kings might be strong enough to capture the pot too. Although pairing your ace or king is no guarantee of winning, your hand is much more valuable than it would be if completing your flush was the only way you could win the pot.

Suppose you flopped T♥-4♥-J♣ to go along with your A♥-K♥. Not only would any of nine hearts make the best possible flush, but any of the three remaining queens – the three that are not hearts – will make the best possible straight. And any other ace or king gives you top pair with top kicker.

With more chances of winning, you get more value for each dollar you have wagered.

This particular hand is so good that instead of attempting to complete your draw inexpensively by checking (not adding to the bet) and hoping that everyone else checks too, you might want to bet in order to get more money into the pot.

Betting might even induce your opponents to fold their hands and then you'll win without even having to get lucky. Between your chances of making a flush with one of the nine hearts presently unaccounted for, and making a straight with any of the other three queens – we've already counted the queen of hearts as one of the nine hearts, so we can't count it twice – there are a dozen cards that can give you the best possible hand. And if a pair of aces or a pair of kings would win the pot, you've got an additional six cards to help you too.

But things aren't always clean and simple, not even in this case. An ace or king means it's possible for one of your other opponents to make a straight too, so a card you think will win the pot for you might not. The only way of sidestepping this is to learn how to decipher what your opponents have.

If the ten of hearts were replaced by a low heart, you wouldn't have a straight draw, but then again, neither would any of your opponents. With a flop of 2♥-7♥-J♣, any ace or king stands a very good chance of helping you, while the chances of that card helping an opponent even more are almost nil.

There's a lot of food for thought here, but at the end of the day it's important to realize that you can usually play drawing hands aggressively whenever you're likely to win the pot by pairing your overcards as well as by completing your draw.

Tip 2

Betting For Value

Winning players make their opponents pay for the chance to draw a card that might give them the best hand. Any time you have the best hand and your opponent can't win the pot without improving, your job is to make it pricey for him.

Without a price to be paid in order to see another card, no hand is too much of a long shot. Even if the odds were 45-to-1 against your opponent – a situation that arises on the turn when there's only one card in the deck that can help him – he has nothing to lose if he can draw for free.

A free card gives him infinite odds, and while a 45-to-1 shot doesn't sound like much, just remember this: he'll fold his hand when it doesn't improve, and won't invest another penny in the pot – but when he miraculously makes his hand, you'll bet, he'll raise, you'll call and your opponent will wind up winning the entire pot with a hand he would have folded had you decided to charge him any sort of reasonable price to try and catch a miracle.

In fixed-limit hold'em, the balance between betting and checking can be confusing. Suppose we're playing $6–$12 hold'em and we've reached the turn, where you have a flush draw and I have a pocket pair of aces. You'll win by making a flush. But if your flush draw fizzles out, we'll assume there's no other card you can catch to give you a winning hand.

Suppose there is $21 in the pot by the time I bet on the flop. You are faced with calling a six-dollar bet. You're getting 3.5-to-1 from the pot. If you complete a flush on the turn (fourth card) or the river (final card), you'll bet or raise, secure in the knowledge that you have the best hand. But if you fail to complete your hand, you'll call the turn but fold when I bet the river.

Because the 3.5-to-1 odds offered by the pot exceed the 1.86-to-1 odds against completing your flush on either the turn or the river, continuing to play is your best option. But from my perspective, I'm better off betting and offering you 3.5-to-1 odds than I would be by checking and allowing you to take a free card. While one of us will win and one of us will lose, we each made the best decision available to us under the circumstances, and that's all we could do.

No-limit poker is a horse of a different colour. Rather than being locked into the odds offered by betting a fixed, predetermined sum of money, I can control the odds offered to you by the pot. Suppose I bet $200 into that $21 pot. While the odds against completing your hand are still 1.86-to-1 against completing your flush, the pot odds have been reduced to nearly even money. Now you're forced to fold, or call a $200 wager in order to win a $221 pot. The size of my wager made the relationship between the pot odds and the odds against making your hand topsy-turvy. And even if you were silly enough to call, you'd have to worry about another bet on the turn if the board doesn't appear threatening to me. If I make another bet, you'll only have one opportunity to catch the card you need, and the price you'd have to pay to draw for that long shot would become prohibitive.

You won't show a profit in the long run by calling this bet, and a good player will toss his flush draw away.

Whenever you have what you think is the best hand, you should consider betting for value. You can think about check-raising, but before you do, be sure your opponent will bet if you check, and will call your raise too. If you can't answer 'yes' to each of these questions, betting for value is usually a better idea.

Save check-raising for those occasions when you have a powerful hand and an aggressive opponent who will interpret your check as a sign of weakness and fire a bet into the pot. Suppose you have A-T, the pot hasn't been raised, and the flop is A♠-A♦-T♠. You'd love to see another spade make a flush for an unsuspecting adversary. You'd also like to see someone holding the last ace to pair his side card for a lower full house than yours. He would probably have a lower full house too, since anyone holding A-J, A-Q or A-K probably would have raised before the flop.

In these rare instances you can afford to give a free card to your opponent in hopes that he improves to the second best hand. But most of the time, betting for value increases the price your opponent is forced to pay if he wants to draw a card to beat you.

Tip 3

Hope

Sometimes you'll look at your cards and find a big, fat, juicy pocket pair of queens or maybe A-K staring back at you. You're thinking, 'I just can't wait to raise.' It's a great feeling – unless someone else raises before it's your turn to act.

Now you're faced with cold-calling two bets instead of seizing the initiative for yourself, and you've got to think about your opponent's hand too. Maybe he's got a pocket pair of kings or aces, and you just went from a big favourite to a long shot in a hurry. But maybe he raised on a whim, or with a marginal hand like Q-J. Players do that all the time, and if he has, your foot is firmly planted on his throat.

An opponent's raise always puts you to the test. Do you step deftly out of the way by folding, should you call, or should you re-raise? Even if you have a big hand, unless it's a pocket pair of aces it might not be the best hand right now. But things might not be that bad. Even if your opponent's hand is stronger, you can always get lucky on the flop. Re-raising now might even allow you to seize the initiative on the next betting round, especially if your opponent was raising with A-K, A-Q or A-J, and the flop misses him entirely.

If that is the case, you can bet if you think you own the best hand, or if you believe a wager might convince your opponent to fold. If you're not sure where you stand after the flop, but your opponent checks, you can check behind him and take a free card.

While raising or folding is usually preferable, you might just want to call in situations where you have a good-but-not-great hand. With powerful hands like K-K or A-A, however, re-raising is always the best choice.

If a solid player raises and you have A-T or K-J – hands that look good under most circumstances – you are better off folding because your opponent will usually have a stronger hand than yours. He probably holds a pair of tens or higher, or two high cards that include an ace. Any ace in his hand probably has a king or queen

27

along with it. If you each have an ace but he has a better kicker, your hand is dominated. Because you need to pair your kicker on the turn or river to win, only three cards in the deck can save you.

If he has a pair, you're either a very slight underdog or a very big one. While a hand like A-T is only a small underdog to a pair of eights, nines or tens, it is a long shot against J-J, Q-Q, K-K or A-A.

Look at the situation realistically. You're a small favourite – almost a coin flip – against some of your opponent's probable hands, a big underdog against others, and dominated to the extent that you have only three outs against others. In the long run you figure to lose a lot of money on those confrontations.

If you're holding a pair of queens, kings or aces, or A-K, you can always re-raise. But with a pair of jacks, you've got a hand that's right on the cusp, and the flop is even money to contain at least one card higher than your jacks.

In a tournament you're really rolling the dice by calling a big raise with a pair of jacks. However, if you're short stacked (have only a few chips), making a stand with a pair of jacks is probably the best thing you can do because it figures to be the best hand you'll see before you're forced to go all-in.

Short stacked tournament players have very few options. You can't wait for a better hand when time is running out. You can't bluff with a short stack because it's an inexpensive opportunity for another player to eliminate an opponent and someone is likely to call. When your back is to the wall and you're completely out of running room, you have no choice. Push all your chips into the centre of the table and hope. It's all you have left at your disposal.

Hope, as you may already have surmised, is the death of many poker players, but in this case no other options are available to you.

Except for running perilously close to empty in a tournament and having little or no manoeuvring room, each tactic you employ in a poker game should be part of a rational plan. And any plan, no matter how dicey it may be, is better than hope.

When you play poker, you may want to heed the words of Dante's *The Divine Comedy*, written 700 years ago: 'All hope abandon, ye who enter here.'

Tip 4   Why it's Important to Know and Understand the Odds

Knowing the odds is a necessary part of any poker player's game. Without this knowledge there's no way to tell whether the money in the pot is sufficient to overcome the odds against making your hand. It's all part of poker's fundamental relationship: how much will it cost to keep playing this hand and how much money am I likely to win if I catch the card I need?

By understanding how the chances of making your hand relates to the money you'll win if you get lucky, you can play skilful, high-percentage poker, instead of treating the game like some form of gambling or lottery.

The process is not difficult. It involves comparing the number of cards that will complete your hand – your outs – with the total number of unknown cards remaining in the deck and then doing a bit of division.

Tip 26 (see page 81) takes you through some of the basic arithmetic required to figure the odds for common situations and provides a chart with many of the odds and outs you need to know when you're playing poker. There's nothing wrong with jumping forward and reading that tip as soon as you finish this one, or you can simply work your way through the book and get to it later.

When push comes to shove, poker is really all about recognizing when the odds against making a winning hand are more than offset by the size of the pot you are likely to win if you make your hand. It's also about taking control of certain situations by knowing when to bet or raise in order to eliminate opponents and increase your chances of winning. But to do this, you have to be able to recognize situations when your chances of winning are increased by bold action on your part.

There are other occasions when you'll want to do whatever you can to keep the pot small and keep as many opponents as possible in the pot with you. This is generally done by playing passively, and is usually the course of action called for when you're trying to complete a difficult draw to a very big hand – a flush, or a full-house, for example – which figures to win a big pot if you get lucky. But because the odds against making that hand are rather long, your ideal strategy is to complete the hand on the cheap by keeping your investment in the pot to a minimum whenever you can.

If you memorize the odds against making various hands – there's a chart in Tip 26 to help you (see page 82) – you won't ever have to do arithmetic at the poker table. All you have to do is count.

You have to count the number of bets going into the pot in order to get a handle on whether the prize is worth the risk. In a fixed limit game, you can either count the bets before and on the flop as half-bets, and the double bets on the turn and river as full bets. In a no-limit game, you'll have to count – or closely estimate – the amount of money going into the pot in order to compare it to the size of a bet you have to call to keep playing.

My own preference in a fixed-limit game is to count the bets before the flop and on the flop as single betting units. Then, before wagering begins on the turn, I divide those bets by two, so the smaller betting units are in units equivalent to the larger betting units on the last two rounds of wagering.

It's easy. Say eight small bets are in the pot by the time wagering begins on the turn. I divide by two and am thinking, 'four bets in the pot'. I add the wagers on the turn to those six full bets. If there are two bets on the turn, my total is six. If I have to call a single bet on the turn, the pot is offering me 6-to-1 odds to do so. If I am trying to make a flush, the pot odds of 6-to-1 will exceed the odds against completing my flush (look at the chart in Tip 26 to see for yourself) and my decision is easy.

It pays to call this bet, and money will be made in the long run by calling bets whenever the pot odds offset the odds against making a hand that figures to win the pot. If you were to repeat this situation time after time, you'll come out ahead in the long run. While you may not make your flush this hand, that's not important in the grand scheme of things. What matters most is that when the payoff exceeds the cost of your risk, it pays to play.

Tip 5

Figure the Odds in Tournaments

In tournaments you have one additional factor to consider when deciding whether to fold or draw. Even when the pot's size offsets the odds against making your hand, the risk might overshadow any potential rewards.

Because the chance of elimination often exceeds any gains you'd realize from winning a hand, it sometimes pays to fold even when the relationship between the pot odds and those against making your hand would ordinarily be favourable.

If you are confronting a bet that will put you all-in, with no more chips to bet, your entire tournament life is at stake, while winning an all-in confrontation seldom comes with any guarantees. You might not even make it to the money. Tournaments are very different from cash games, and tournament decisions must sometimes be made with an eye to your relative position against the entire field. That's never an issue in a cash game, when all that's at stake is winning or losing the money wagered on that hand.

Tournament players also have to consider the relationship between their chip count and the cost to play one complete orbit of poker. Early in a tournament most players usually have a very large amount of chips compared to the blinds.

In a tournament where players begin with $1,500 in chips and blinds of $10–20, it costs only $30 in blinds to play one full orbit of poker, and each player has 50 times that in chips. Because each player has lots of chips compared to the blinds, the early stages of tournaments can be played much like cash games. Draws to straights and flushes are playable now, but will become unplayable later on in the event, when the blinds have escalated and a player may only have four, five or ten times the cost of a round of blinds.

Playing a drawing hand in those circumstances is likely to involve going all-in, risking your entire tournament life in a situation where it's usually a lot better to play a made hand than a draw.

Nevertheless, there are lots of tournament circumstances where you have to risk your entire tournament life on marginal hands. If you have a relatively small stack of chips, you can't afford to sit and wait for a big pocket pair. They don't come around often enough. That means going all-in with as little as a lone ace – especially when no one else has voluntarily entered the pot yet and you still have enough chips to make one of your opponents think twice about calling your all-in bet.

In these situations, calculating outs is not terribly important. What matters most is deciding whether you believe your all-in bet stands a good chance of winning the pot right there, coupled with your chances of having the best hand right now and your chances of winning if you pair your ace.

Pot odds do become important in tournaments when you have a hand with a draw attached to it. You might flop a pair with a draw, giving you two ways to win. When that happens, you can't ignore those additional outs that your draw offers. You might pick up a draw while holding two cards bigger than the board. If you pair one of your overcards (cards of a higher rank than the board cards), you might win without ever having to make your draw.

If you take one thing away from this particular tip, it's this: In a tournament, the relationship between the size of the pot and the odds against making your hand isn't the same as it is in a cash game. In a cash game, each hand is a world unto itself, played in a vacuum. But in tournament poker, each hand must be analyzed and assessed in terms of chip counts, relative stack size compared to the cost of playing another orbit of hands, where you stand in relationship to your opponent's chip count, and whether playing and winning will move you up the pay ladder.

You've got to take a different look at things when making a play-or-fold decision in a tournament, and that look is much broader than it is in a cash game.

Tip 6

Figure the Implied Odds

Whenever all the cards have been dealt and you're the last player to act, it pays to call – by matching – the previous bet if your chances of winning exceed the odds the pot offers you. Otherwise, folding makes more sense. If you figure to win once in three times when the pot offers 5-to-1 odds, calling pays regardless of whether you win this particular hand or not. It's the long run that matters in poker, not the outcome of any given hand.

But on earlier betting rounds, when there are still more cards to be dealt, more players to act, and more betting rounds to come, it's difficult to know precisely how much it will cost to try to make your hand because you can never be sure how the betting will proceed or how many opponents will stick around and pay you off if you make the winning hand.

That's where *implied odds* come into play. Implied odds are the ratio of what you should win – including money likely to be bet in subsequent rounds – to the cost of a current bet. Implied odds are really an educated guess, since one never knows how many opponents will remain in the hunt or how much money will be wagered on future betting rounds.

Implied odds are affected by a number of factors. They're better when your hand is hidden because your opponents might not realize what you have and pay you off with lesser hands. That's why a set – a pair in your hand that matches the rank of one of the community cards, giving you three of a kind – is usually more profitable than a pair on the board that matches a third card of that rank in your hand.

Betting structures affect implied odds too. Pot-limit and no-limit games, with their potential for huge wagers, offer greater implied odds than a fixed-limit game.

Your opponents' playing styles can also increase or reduce implied odds. Players who call but seldom bet or raise increase implied odds, because you can draw inexpensively against them, knowing all the while you'll get paid off if you make your hand.

The amount of money already in the pot is another reason you might want to continue playing a hand even when you're not the favourite. Here's why. If you flop a four-flush, the odds are 1.86-to-1 against completing your hand. You might even make your flush and still lose. Even though you are not favoured to win the hand, you may still be a *money favourite*. In other words, even if you only win just once every three times you find yourself in that situation, it pays to draw as long as the pot promises to return two dollars or more for each dollar you have to pay to draw to your flush.

While there are always caveats that might cause you to deviate from these suggestions, here are three rules of thumb to think about when you're considering the pot odds/implied odds relationship.

✓ If you are a money favourite on new money – forget about any money already in the pot – bet or raise to build the pot. For example, if you've flopped a flush draw, are last to act, and four players have already called, go ahead and raise. The odds against completing your hand are only 1.86-to-1 against you, but you're getting 4-to-1 on *new money* wagered on that round and you should bet or raise to build a bigger pot.

✓ If you are a money favourite due to the size of the pot plus any implied odds you think will accrue if you make your hand, calling is usually the best option. If you ignore the fact that raising may allow you to win the pot by causing your opponents to fold, raising reduces your implied odds.

✓ If you have neither pot odds nor implied odds, and are not a money favourite, fold and save your money.

When Oscar Wilde wrote, 'The pure and simple truth is rarely pure and never simple,' he wasn't thinking about a poker game, but his words hold true nonetheless. These three rules of thumb are not the entire answer and, although it's easy to come up with reasons to deviate from them on occasion, the fact remains that the relationship between pot odds, implied odds, the odds against making your hand, and money that's already in the pot, will go a long way towards answering that age-old poker conundrum: shall I check or bet, or fold, call or raise?

Tip 7 Choosing the Right Online Game

You won't always be able to use this tip, but whenever you can use it, it promises to be a jewel. In smaller casinos and cardrooms, you might only find one game available at the betting limits you prefer. When that's the case, your only choice is to play the available game or not play at all.

But in larger casinos, whenever you have a choice of games at your preferred betting limits, and online – where there are usually a number of games to choose from – picking the best game can be the most important decision you'll make during that session.

Choosing a good game isn't difficult at all, as long as you know what to look for. And what you're looking for is an elevated fun factor. Players who are there to have fun are usually not as serious about the game. For these players, a good time – a night out at the casino, even if it's a night of online poker – usually takes precedence over tight, tactical play and winning money.

So look for the fun factor. It's easy to find. Players who are drinking, laughing, chatting, flirting or engaging in any of the myriad possible activities unrelated to the game at hand are the very players you're looking for.

It also helps if they have lots of chips on the table – a sure sign they've come to gamble. On the other hand, you'll want to avoid tables where there is a low fun factor or none at all, where everyone is deadly serious and concentrating on poker to the exclusion of everything else. If most of the players seem to be short on chips, that's even worse. Even if you were to have a spectacularly good run of cards, there isn't all that much money on the table for you to win.

If you're playing online you won't know if anyone is drinking or has come to socialize and flirt at the expense of playing poker, but there are plenty of clues at your disposal to help you decide whether you're in a good game or not.

Most of these clues can be found in your online site's lobby. Check the average size of the pot, and the number of players who typically see the flop. Bigger pots usually mean looser play, but not always. You'll want to avoid games where a relatively few number of players see the flop but the average pot is quite large. This is a sure sign of a very aggressive game, with frequent raising before the flop. In games like this it can cost quite a bit to see the flop, which is not always going to be to your liking.

However, the more players per flop, the more certain you can be that you have found a loose game. If you find a game with a relatively large number of players seeing the flop, but with moderately sized pots, you can be sure you've found a loose, passive game – and those are the easiest games to beat.

Once you bring up the online room, pay attention to the chat function. If you see a lot of chatter going back and forth, it's another sign of a very social game. It also may be a sign that these players know each other very well, probably from playing together on a regular basis. And while they won't know your style very well, they will be familiar with each other's play.

There are pluses and minuses to this, but if you're in a chatty game, where raising is infrequent but there are lots of players in each hand, you've found a good game.

Tip 8

Starting Standards

Most poker theorists have devoted quite a bit of thought and effort to starting hand standards. After all, deciding which hands are playable and which ought to be tossed in the muck is a key decision, and most other decisions made during the play of a hand can usually be traced back to the cards you chose to enter the pot with.

Most of the starting hands experts recommend playing are quite similar, and in any event, there are no contrarian theorists out there arguing that you ought to play 9-2 offsuit under the gun. What is important is that winning play requires following some set of standards, especially if you are new to the game.

Choosing your hands is a critical decision in limit hold'em games because fixed-limit betting structures are all about capitalizing on small, repeatable edges time after time.

Because you won't have any idea about how many players will be in the pot with you when you're in early position, you need to play strong hands – the kind that figure to play well regardless of whether you're facing a lone opponent or an entire army.

In later position, when you know how many opponents will be involved in the hand, deciding whether you should play a drawing hand – the kind that usually requires a number of opponents before they're potentially worthwhile – is much easier. Because these hands are infrequent winners, it takes a large pot to overcome the cost of all those drawing hands that never worked out.

Selecting starting hands in no-limit hold'em is often more a case of stack size than the number of opponents. You can play hands that won't win frequently as long as you and your opponent have lots of chips. Because you're looking for situations where you can win all your opponent's chips, you don't necessarily need a lot of opponents in the pot with you. In a fixed-limit game, the only way to build a big pot is to have a large number of adversaries contributing to the pot. But in no-limit poker, as long as you and your opponent each have a large number of chips, you can win a big hand even if just the two of you are contesting it.

A hand you might even throw away in a limit game can become a keeper in a no-limit game. Let's assume you have a small pocket pair and someone raised in early position. You're a 7.5-to-1 underdog to flop a set, and because you probably won't win this hand unless you improve, your best play is to fold before the flop. But you can call a modest raise in a no-limit game, as long as both of you have a large amount of chips. If you flop a set it will be well disguised and you might win all your opponent's chips. Even if you don't, you should usually win enough to compensate for those occasions when he raised and you called with a small pair but failed to improve on the flop and had to release your hand when your opponent bet.

Choosing a starting hand in limit hold'em is often related to the cost of playing and the number of opponents in the pot with you. But in no-limit hold'em, the overriding factor is frequently based on the number of chips each of you have. For fixed-limit hold'em, here are some suggested starting hands (see table opposite).

How closely you adhere to these standards should depend on your experience level. Standards should be the gospel for beginners, a helpful guide for skilled players, and simply a point of departure for experts.

Once you know enough about the game to recognize appropriate opportunities, you can deviate whenever your adjustment represents a more profitable play. It doesn't supplant the *book play*; it simply means that for a specific situation, you've found an even more profitable alternative.

If you're a beginning hold'em player, adhering to these standards may seem boring and repetitive, but for the time being, you'll win more money by playing boring, repetitive poker than you would by looking for reasons to deviate from the book move.

Skilled players can use these standards as a guide rather than as the gospel. You'll still be playing by the book most of the time, and only deviating enough to put some variety into your game and some doubt into the minds of your opponents. Even in no-limit hold'em you can use these starting hand standards as a guide, as long as you

Starting Hand Standards for Fixed-limit Hold'em Games

Playable hands in early position (first four positions to the dealer's left)	
Pairs:	Sevens through to aces
Suited:	Aces with a king, queen, jack or ten
	King with a queen, jack or ten
	Queen with a jack or ten
	Jack with a ten or nine
	Ten with a nine
Unsuited:	Aces with a king, queen, jack or ten
	King with a queen or jack
Playable hands in middle position (positions five, six and seven)	
Pairs:	Fives and sixes
Suited:	Aces with a nine, eight, seven or six
	King with a nine
	Queen with a nine or eight
	Jack with an eight
	Ten with an eight
	Nine with an eight
Unsuited:	King with a ten
	Queen with a jack or ten
	Jack with a ten
Playable hands in late position (positions eight, nine and ten)	
Pairs:	Fours, treys and deuces
Suited:	Aces with a five, four, three or two
	King with an eight, seven, six, five, four, three or two
	Jack with a seven
	Ten with a seven
	Nine with a seven or six
	Eight with a seven or six
	Seven with a six or five
	Six with a five
	Five with a four
Unsuited:	King with a nine
	Queen with a nine
	Jack with a nine or eight
	Ten with a nine or eight
	Nine with an eight or seven
	Eight with a seven

remember that relative stack size – the number of chips each player has in front of him – is at least as important as the intrinsic strength of a hand.

Without starting standards to guide you, you'll never be able to put together a cogent plan. And whenever you make a move at the poker table without much of a plan, you usually don't have much of a prayer either.

Tip 9

Making Adjustments to Starting Standards

Poker is a game of adjustments, and good players always make tactical adjustments to their play based on what opponents are doing and the general texture of the game. If our adversaries are savvy and play well, they're adjusting to us too. Adjusting to us as we adjust to them sounds like a complex series of negotiations or a smooth-as-silk dance team, seamlessly making something difficult look easy.

You'll have to make adjustments at the poker table too, particularly where your starting hands are concerned. Some hands that are playable in a passive game, where there's a lot more calling than raising, are hands that are better off folded when the game turns overly aggressive.

What's the best way to adjust to a very aggressive game? If most pots are raised before the flop, you can no longer play hands such as mid-range suited connectors unless you can see the flop for just one bet. These hands lose a lot of value when pots are frequently raised and the field is usually narrowed.

Drawing hands such as mid-range suited connectors not only require large pots to be potentially profitable, but you have to be able to see the flop inexpensively too. You can't afford to invest too much money in the pot with drawing hands because you'll throw the vast majority of them away once you see the flop. Because you'll seldom throw away a big pocket pair of queens, kings or aces on the flop, you can invest more money in these hands early on.

If someone raises before it's your turn to act and you know this opponent raises far more often than his cards really warrant, you can – and should – re-raise with any pair of tens or higher. You can also re-raise with A-K and A-Q. However, hands like T-9 suited ought to be folded. After all, a hand like T-9 suited needs a lot of players to make it a good investment. Most of your equity with speculative hands like these comes from making a straight or a flush, and you need a lot of customers and an inexpensive flop to wrest the intrinsic value from drawing hands like these.

Regardless of the two cards you've been dealt, the flop won't help you about two-thirds of the time. Although you'll occasionally flop a huge hand when you play T-9 suited, most of the time you'll be left with an unimproved ten-high, and that's not going to win very many pots.

In a tough, aggressive game, here's a recommended list of playable hands. If you compare this chart to the one in the preceding chapter, you'll see that far fewer hands are recommended in tough, aggressive games.

Starting Hand Standards for Tough, Aggressive Fixed-limit Hold'em Games

Playable hands in early position (first four positions to the dealer's left)	
Pairs:	Sevens through aces
Suited:	Aces with a king or queen
	King with a queen
	Queen with a jack
Unsuited:	Aces with a king or queen
	King with a queen
Playable hands in middle position (positions five, six and seven)	
Pairs:	Fives and sixes
Suited:	Aces with a jack or ten
	King with a jack or ten
	Jack with a ten
Unsuited:	Aces with a jack
	King with a jack
	Queen with a jack
Playable hands in late position (positions eight, nine and ten)	
Pairs:	Fours, treys, and deuces
Suited:	Aces with a nine
	Queen with a ten
	King with a nine
	Jack with a nine
	Ten with an nine or eight
	Nine with an eight
Unsuited:	Aces with a ten
	King with a ten
	Jack with a ten
	Ten with a nine

Hands in this chart can be played only if the pot has not been raised when it's your turn to act. If there is a raise before it's your turn to act, and the price to see the flop is now two bets, you can re-raise with any pair of jacks, queens, kings or aces, as well as with A-K and A-Q, but fold everything else.

If this seems overly restrictive, consider that most good fixed-limit hold'em players will raise with any pair of nines or higher, as well as with A-K, A-Q A-J or K-Q, and frequently A-T and K-J. If you follow these suggestions, you'll be re-raising with hands that reside at the top of your opponent's raising spectrum while folding all others. That gives you a fighting chance of having the best hand when you re-raise, without putting yourself into the unenviable position of re-raising only to find that your hand is a large underdog.

In a no-limit game, you can call a modest raise of perhaps three to four times the size of the big blind as long as you and your opponent each have a substantial amount of chips. But to do so, you'll need a high-potential hand. Calling a raise in a no-limit game with A-J leaves you very vulnerable to anyone who raised with a big pocket pair or with a hand like A-K. If it's the latter you need to pair your jack, and only three of them remain in the deck. The rest of the deck belongs to your opponent. When you have three outs, you are said to be dominated. And when you are dominated, you really shouldn't risk a gamble when you're a significant underdog on the flop.

But if you call with a pair, your decision is easy: either flop a set (which occurs when a card appears on the flop that is the same rank as your pair, giving you three-of-a-kind) or fold. There's no guarantee that flopping a set means you'll win the pot, but it stands a much better chance than flopping a pair or two. After all, if your opponent makes a big bet and you've got a lot of chips in front of you, it's usually inadvisable to risk them all on one pair.

If either you or your opponent only has a small stack, you can go all-in with top pair, because you won't have all that much at risk. (Top pair is a pair made with the highest ranking community card and one of the cards in your hand.)

Tip 10

Pay Attention to Your Side Card

In a game that features communal cards that all players must use to make their hands, it's not unusual for two hold'em players to end up with hands that are identical except for their unpaired side cards. It's your side card, or *kicker*, which often spells the difference between winning or losing a pot.

The reason A-K is regarded as a big hand while A-2 is better thrown away the majority of the time is the strength of the kicker. If you flop a pair with A-K, it is guaranteed to be the highest possible pair with the best possible kicker. But with A-2, you'll flop either a pair of aces with the worst possible kicker or a pair of deuces that seldom figures to be the best hand, regardless of the fact that its side card is an ace.

Let's walk through an example. Suppose you've been dealt A-Q and I have A-5. If the flop is A-4-4, we've each made two pair. And if things ended right here, you would win based on the strength of your kicker. After all, A-A-4-4-Q is a better hand than A-A-4-4-5.

I can only win by catching a five on the turn or the river. And if I did, my A-A-5-5-4 would beat your A-A-4-4-Q. It's a long shot, because I have to catch one of the three remaining fives in the deck. No other cards in the deck can help me win, though there are a few that would force a tied hand and we'd split the pot. For example, if a king were to fall, we'd both have A-A-4-4-K, and your previously superior queen kicker would be sidelined by the communal king. Because it's shared by both of us, we'd each have an identical hand and the pot would be split neatly in half.

Sometimes the kicker comes into play even when there isn't a pair on board. Suppose the board read A-9-8-7-2 at hand's end. With your A-Q, you'd hold A-A-Q-9-8. With my A-5, the best hand I could make from my two private cards and the five board cards would be A-A-9-8-7. My five is so pitifully small that it wouldn't even play. Your pair of aces with a queen kicker would take the pot while my pair of aces with its sorry kicker would be kicked to the curb.

That's why most savvy players throw away two-card holdings with weak kickers. With a weak kicker you're never quite as sure how you stack up during the play of the hand. As a result, you're frequently relegated to passive play. Even if you win with a hand like A-5, it will probably be less than you would have won by aggressively betting a hand like A-K all the way to the river.

Although never desirable, weak side cards are worse with an ace in your hand than they are with any other card in the deck. Here's why. Many of your opponents love aces and will eagerly play any ace they are dealt. They won't do that with any other card.

Hands like K-3 or Q-5 are seldom played – even the weakest of your opponents learn to throw them away – but some of your opponents will play hands like A-5 and A-3 regularly.

If you play a weak king and are fortunate enough to catch a king on the flop, you stand a pretty good chance of being the only player holding a pair of kings. Your odds are even better if the pot was not raised before the flop – thus minimizing the chances that anyone was dealt such obvious raising hands as A-K, K-Q or K-J.

But when you play a weak ace, the implications can be horrific. You're likely to find that someone else holds an ace too. And while his kicker might be weak, it's probably better than a trey or a deuce. Even if you jump into the pot with a middle-of-the-road kicker like A-7 or A-8, you won't have any idea whether yours is the best hand.

That's kicker trouble. It's an occupational disease of poker players. It happens to everyone. Even the very best players run into it every now and then, but you can minimize its chances of striking you. If you're playing A-Q, the only way you can run into kicker trouble is if your opponent was dealt A-K. There's a lot less likelihood of that happening than if you decide to play A-3 or A-4 and run into another player who was fortunate enough to be dealt an ace too.

Tip 11

Adjusting to the Number of Opponents

One of poker's enduring dilemmas is what to do when you start off with a big, promising hand like A-K only to see the air go out of your balloon when the flop provides no help at all. Imagine that you raised before the flop with A-K only to see a disappointing 9-5-3 flop. What should you do now?

As long as you're able to count to three, no additional skills are required to resolve this dilemma. Against only one or two other players, your A-K may be the best hand right now – and on the river too – regardless of whether the flop helped your hand or missed it altogether. But if you are facing three opponents or more, you need to be extremely careful.

Against three or more players, a flop that doesn't help you probably helps someone else. And the more opponents who are competing against you for the pot, the more likely this is to be true. An unimproved A-K might still stand a semblance of a chance against three or even four opponents, though it's not worth betting on. But against six, seven or eight opponents, your chances will progressively diminish and you won't stand a chance of winning the pot without a really good hand.

When the flop doesn't help you, *fit or fold* is the best course of action. If you need a measure to guide you, the break-off point is three opponents. Against one or two opponents you might win even when big cards like A-K don't improve. Against three opponents or more, you're usually better off saving your money and going on to the next hand.

As a general rule, the more opponents in the pot, the more straightforward poker you should play. Overcards (cards of a higher rank than the communal cards on the board) are unlikely to win against a large number of opponents. To win with an unimproved A-K, you'll need to catch an ace or king on the turn or the river while hoping it does not give an opponent two pair. You also have to hope you are not up against a better hand already. If that's the case, you're *drawing dead* by continuing to invest more money in a pot that you have no chance of winning.

Deciding whether you're up against two pair is not as tough as it sounds, and it doesn't require any mind-reading ability. Just look at the flop's texture. The chances that an opponent made two pair are greater with a flop like 10-9-7 or J-10-9 than they would be if the flop were J-6-3. And here's the reason why. The majority of your opponents will play connected cards, such as 7-8, but most of them will correctly eschew playing absolutely ragged hands such as J-6, J-3 or 6-3.

If you stick around with an unimproved A-K and are fortunate enough to pair-up on the turn, you stand a good chance of winning if the flop was J-6-3. Although you still might win if the flop is J-10-9, your chances are diminished because the flop's composition supports the potential for hands such as two pair or a straight.

You also need to count your opponents before attempting a bluff. The more opponents, the less bluffing you can do. It's nearly impossible to bluff seven players, and foolish to try. After all, the flop that missed you probably hit one of your opponents, and he's the one who will call your bet. But if you are up against only one or two opponents, you might be able to steal the pot often enough to make a propitious bluff pay off.

If you're thinking of trying a bluff, make sure you have two opponents or fewer and that they are players who have already shown a willingness to fold marginal hands. Even if you are confronting just one opponent, a bluff is doomed to fail if he fancies himself the table sheriff, and is bound and determined not to let anyone steal a pot from him.

Tip 12

Calling from the Small Blind

Although there's some good news associated with playing the blinds, the sad truth is that you'll lose money over the course of your lifetime when it's your turn in the blinds. That's true regardless of how well you play, and the reason is *position*.

You have the benefit of acting last before the flop, but then you have to act before all your opponents on each of the three succeeding rounds. When you act first, you won't know whether someone will raise if you bet, or bet if you check. You won't even know how many opponents will play the pot with you.

This is critical information. If you have no idea about how good a hand an opponent might have – or might represent – it's tough to decide what your best course of action should be. Without knowing how many opponents you'll face, you're forced to guess about whether you will be getting the right number of callers to overcome the odds against making your hand.

In a ten-handed game you'll be in the blind 20 per cent of the time. In a shorthanded game – such as the six-handed games that are so popular online – you're going to have to make a forced blind bet over 33 per cent of the time.

Losing money over the course of your lifetime from those positions is not an encouraging prospect. However, the saving grace is that your opponents have their turn in the barrel too. If you can reduce the amount you lose in the blinds, you'll do just fine in the end.

When you are in the blinds, you ought to think more about saving bets than winning pots. If you have a weak hand in the blind there's usually very little you can do, particularly in a fixed-limit game, to overcome a good player with a better hand.

Deciding whether to commit more money to the pot means that you will have to ask yourself the question 'Does your hand have a positive expectation in the long run?' If it does, keep playing. If it doesn't, save your money and fold.

The size of the blind plays a role in determining whether to call from the small blind or release your hand. In most fixed-limit games the small blind is half the size of the big blind. But in games like $15–$30, $3–$6 or the small blind is either one-third or two-thirds of the big blind. In a $15–$30 game the small blind is $10, but in a $3–$6 game it is usually $1. Although there's no standard rule, the amount needed to complete the blind bears heavily on whether or not to complete your bet if no one has raised.

With only one voluntary caller you can raise with any pair of sevens or higher, any two cards ten or higher, and any suited connectors as low as T-9. Your raise is an attempt to eliminate the big blind in order to contest the pot heads up with you in the lead against the caller, who presumably has a hand too weak to raise. But if he re-raises, or even just calls, and you miss the flop, it's time to fold and avoid a big loss.

With two or three players already in the pot, you ought to raise with A-A, K-K, Q-Q, as well as with A-K and A-Q. You probably have the best hand and increasing the size of the pot is the goal of this raise. But there's a risk to raising with A-K and A-Q. You have to come out betting regardless of the flop and without any knowledge about how it might have affected your opponents. Although raising with pocket pairs of aces, kings or queens is always a good idea, you might want to keep your foot off the accelerator with hands like A-K until you see the flop and have some idea about the quality of your hand.

You can complete the small blind with any two cards when the cost to do so is only one-third of a bet. In most games, where the small blind is half of a bet, you can complete the bet holding any pair, any two suited cards of 5-4 or higher, and any connectors and one-gap hands of 7-6 or better. In a $3–$6 game, where the cost to complete the blind is two-thirds of a bet, complete the small blind only when you have a hand you'd play from most other positions.

With a *family pot* composed of six or more players including the blinds, you can raise with smaller pairs. Your objective is to create a big pot, because the size of the pot will almost certainly offset the odds against making your hand. If you flop a set, it's always well hidden and you can count on getting paid off by your opponents. If you miss your set, and the flop contains some cards bigger than your pair and there's any appreciable action, you can fold.

Tip 13
Hands You Can Play in Any Position Before the Flop

Before the flop, each of the 169 unique starting combinations can be neatly placed into one of five categories: pairs, connecting cards, gapped cards, suited connectors or suited gapped cards.

If you weren't dealt a pair your cards will either be suited or unsuited and either connected or gapped. Gapped cards in general are not as valuable as connected cards because of their difficulty in completing straights. The smaller the gap, the easier it is to make a straight, with the exception of cards at the top or bottom of the deck, such as A-Q, K-J, 4-2 and the like. These hands won't make as many straights because there are fewer possible cards to connect with them. The same is true for connected cards at the top or bottom of the deck. Although A-K is a terrific starting hand, it can only make a straight with Q-J-T, whereas a hand like J-T can make a straight with A-K-Q, K-Q-9, Q-9-8, and 9-8-7.

A general guideline is to play few hands in early position. Cards that aren't suited or paired, or that are three-gapped or more, should be released under most circumstances. Remember, suited cards are more valuable than unsuited cards, given they are of equal rank. Acting late in a hand is a big advantage. You can afford to see the flop with weaker hands in late position. You won't go wrong if you choose to play very few hands in early position.

You can generally play any pair from aces through to sevens in early position, and you can always raise with kings, queens or aces. If you are in late position against a large number of opponents and no one has raised, calling with a lower pair, such as sevens or eights, is really a drawing hand of sorts. You are hoping to flop a set. Sets are always well hidden and you'll have lots of customers to pay you off if you get lucky. In a no-limit game you might be able to take all of your opponent's chips if you flop a set and he's willing to gamble with two pair or less.

In late position, when no one has raised, you can raise with any pair in hopes of playing against only one of the blinds. Your pair is probably the best hand against just one opponent, and you have the advantage of acting last in the three subsequent rounds of betting.

Hands such as A-K, A-Q, A-J and A-T are premium *draws,* not premium hands. However, many players treat them – A-K suited in particular – as though they are as valuable as a pair of aces or kings. The difference? A pair has immediate value. With a drawing hand, all you have is potential – potential that will not always be realized.

If you hold an A-T or A-J in early position and the pot is raised before it's your turn to act, throw them away. You probably have a weaker hand than the raiser. In fact, if you choose not to play hands like these from early position in aggressive games that feature frequent raises before the flop, you'll save money.

In a tournament or no-limit cash game, these hands are even more vulnerable. All of your chips are potentially at risk and you can't afford to jeopardize them when all you have is, say, one pair.

Things get frustrating when you're one of the four players seated to the immediate left of the player with the dealer button. Most of the time you'll simply throw away the cards you've been dealt. If selectivity is one of the hallmarks of strong hold'em players, it is an absolute prerequisite for successful play in early position.

Here's a list of recommended starting hands from early position. Even this short list leans towards the liberal side, and if you're in a game that's aggressive, or in a no-limit hold'em tournament, you can drop A-J, A-T, K-J, K-T, Q-T, J-9 and T-9 from the list, unless you're playing in a very passive game.

Playable hands in early position

Pairs:	Sevens through aces
Suited:	Aces with a king, queen, jack or ten
	King with a queen, jack or ten
	Queen with a jack or ten
	Jack with a ten or nine
	Ten with a nine
Unsuited:	Aces with a king, queen, jack or ten
	King with a queen or jack

Tip 14 — Hands You Can Play in Middle Position Before the Flop

You can loosen up a bit when four or more players have acted before you because you've had the benefit of seeing those opponents reveal the real or purported strength of their hands. In middle position your chances of facing a raise have lessened somewhat and you have more of an indication about how your opponents will play their hands.

In a tame game you can add sixes and fives to your repertoire of playable pairs. If the players who act after you raise frequently, then you should change games, change seats or constrict the range of hands you play, because pairs like sevens and eights, never mind sixes and fives, don't fare very well in raised pots.

If you're the only one confronting the blinds, you can play your pair of sixes as though it was a pair of kings and hope that it survives as the best hand, or that your opponents fold. Against three or more opponents your objective on the flop is to hit a set or fold if big cards appear and there's any appreciable action.

If your opponents routinely play any ace, you can extend your playable repertoire and add A-9 suited through A-6 suited. Against an opponent eager to play any hand with an ace in it, A-9 stands a good chance of being the best hand if no one raised before the flop, because many players will raise with an A-T suited or better in fixed-limit games. But be aware that A-8 through A-6 are dangerous hands because you could flop an ace and find yourself outkicked.

Gapped hands that are suited and some suited *connectors* can look good, but they are far from powerhouses. These include hands such as K-9s, Q-9s, Q-8s, J-8s, T-8s and 9-8s. With the exception of 9-8s they are all gapped and therefore offer fewer straight possibilities than do connected cards. In fact, one of the dangers with this group of starting hands is that they can look good – especially to the uninitiated.

To some degree, knowing how to play such hands separates good poker players from poor ones. Big hands can be played on cruise control and weak ones are easily thrown away. But with hands like these you seldom know where you stand with any degree of certainty; at best you suspect.

When you're in middle position and no one has raised you can play all of the hands recommended for play in early position, and you are welcome to add the hands in the following chart to your repertoire as well.

But remember, if the pot has been raised, or if you have aggressive players who act behind you, or you're in a no-limit tournament or cash game where all your chips can be at risk, please err on the side of conservative play and refrain from getting involved with marginal starting cards.

Playable hands in middle position

Pairs:	Fives and sixes
Suited:	Aces with a nine, eight, seven or six
	King with a nine
	Queen with a nine or eight
	Jack with an eight
	Ten with an eight
	Nine with an eight
Unsuited:	King with a ten
	Queen with a jack or ten
	Jack with a ten

Tip 15

Hands You Can Play in Late Position Before the Flop

In late position you have the advantage of acting last or next to last. As a result, you can add a wide variety of hands to your arsenal. Most of these bargain basement hands should not be played if the pot has been raised when it's your turn to act. Even if you can see the flop inexpensively, playing these hands successfully requires the discipline to release them if the flop brings anything less than an abundant harvest of friendly cards.

Playable hands in late position

Pairs:	Fours, treys and deuces
Suited:	Aces with a five, four, three or two
	King with an eight, seven, six, five, four, three or two
	Jack with a seven
	Ten with a seven
	Nine with a seven or six
	Eight with a seven or six
	Seven with a six or five
	Six with a five
	Five with a four
Unsuited:	King with a nine
	Queen with a nine
	Jack with a nine or eight
	Ten with a nine or eight
	Nine with an eight or seven
	Eight with a seven

When you're on or near the button you can play any pair, providing the pot has not been raised. Go ahead and play deuces, treys and fours. You can play them even if you're up against a large number of opponents and there's no chance you'll have top pair on the flop. Your strategy is simple: release your hand unless you flop a set or an open-ended straight draw.

When you're on the button you can raise with a small pair if no one has called the blinds. You'll be favoured too, albeit slightly, over two random cards. The fact that the blinds might fold, coupled with your chances of flopping a set or simply holding a better hand than your opponents' random cards, makes this play worthwhile.

In late position, with little fear of a raise, you can play hands as weak as A-5s through A-2s. You'd love to flop a flush with this hand, because it would be the nut flush. But if you do not flop a flush or a flush draw, this hand can be fraught with danger. If an ace flops you may be in deep kicker trouble. Even if you make two pair, you might find yourself looking at two bigger pair. An ace with a small kicker tends to win small pots while losing big ones. Play these hands carefully, and release them whenever you suspect your ace might be bested by another ace with a better kicker.

Mid-range connectors such as 9-8 and 8-7 are classic *fit or fold* hands. If you don't flop a big hand or a big draw, you'll simply have to release your hand. Eights and sevens seldom hold up as top pair, and when they do you've always got to worry about a straight draw.

Play these hands cheaply, if you play them at all. Make sure you've got lots of opponents to pay you off on those few occasions when you're fortunate enough to find yourself the recipient of a small miracle on the flop. If you can't play the hand on the cheap, or if you don't think your opponents will pay you off on the river, toss your cards away.

Some of the bargain basement hands you might play in late position are a real tightrope act. Possibilities for winning are limited from the outset, yet the chances of losing a big pot haven't diminished one iota. Play them late, play them in an unraised pot, and fold if you think you're beaten.

Please remember that you can't expect to grow as a player if all you do is follow these starting hand charts without ever deviating from them. While these charts should be the gospel for beginner players, they are a guide for experienced poker players and a point of departure for experts.

Tip 16

Calling a Raise from the Blind

If no one raises your blind bet, consider yourself fortunate. Seeing the flop for free, or for a fractional bet, is some compensation for having to act first on each succeeding round of betting.

It's a different story when an opponent raises. Aside from the situation where no one has called and now a player on or near the button raises – a situation that just screams larceny – a player who raises is announcing that he has a big hand. If you call from one of the blind positions, you'll have to act first on each succeeding betting round.

You can re-raise with a big hand, but if you do this routinely you might be giving your opponents too much information. Raising from the blind is tantamount to announcing to the table that you have an exceptional hand.

Suppose you called from late position with a hand like 9-8 suited and are raised by the big blind. You're plan is to see the flop and then decide whether to keep playing. If the flop is 9-8-4, you've got two pair and it's well hidden. Your opponent in the blind – whose raise was a ringing exclamation that he's likely to be holding a very big pair – is forced to act first on each betting round and he'll have no idea about the strength of your hand until it's too late.

When he bets, you can call the flop and raise on the turn if a safe card falls. Most players in low- to mid-limit games are not going to release aces or kings when they're raised. They'll call even when almost certain they're beaten. In no-limit poker, this is the kind of situation – when you know what your opponent has while he has no idea at all about your hand – where a player with a pocket pair of aces or kings gets eliminated from a tournament or loses his entire stack in a cash game.

Most low- to mid-limit players will not release a big pair. Good no-limit players are willing to release pocket pairs of kings or aces in these situations, but too many others are willing to die with their aces. You can take advantage of this tendency by check-raising from the blind when you know you have the best hand.

Whenever someone checks a big hand in the blind, his opponents will have no idea about its strength. With a free play in the blind, he could have anything. A 7-2 offsuit is as likely as A-K, and a meager pair of deuces is as probable as aces. If the blind holds a big pair and flops a set, he can check the turn, hoping that one of his opponents will bet, which will allow him to check-raise with the certainty that he holds the best hand.

Many players in low- to mid-limit games are reluctant to relinquish their blinds. You simply can't call a raise with a hand like 8-5, even if that raise represents only half a bet to you. On the other hand, if you're holding a hand like K-2 suited, and there are 4 or 5 callers before it is raised, you should call. With four callers you are getting 9-to-1 on your money and you can hope for a miracle even though you will end up releasing your hand most of the time. If you happen to get lucky, your opponents probably won't know how strong your hand is before it's too late.

When you're in the small blind you need an even stronger hand to call a raise because it will cost you more than half a bet. In most games the price is a bet and a half to call a raise from the small blind. In games structured like the $15–$30, the cost is a bet and a third.

Here are some rules of thumb for playing when you're in the blind.

✓ Only play your better hands if it costs you half a bet, but play most of your hands when the cost is only one-third of a bet.

✓ If, as is usually the case, the flop is unfavourable, toss your hand away when someone bets.

✓ If the flop is favourable, tread carefully – you still have the disadvantage of acting first on each succeeding round of betting.

✓ Play very few hands – and play most of them cautiously.

Tip 17

Default Programming

In poker, as in life, we are often prisoners of our own design. We're creatures of habit who are all too prone to repeat the same actions when faced with familiar circumstances, time after time. That can get you into trouble in a poker game.

Most of us have some sort of default programming at work. The majority of poker players will call if they have no specific reason to fold or raise. It's a cautious stance, designed to save money that might be lost on an otherwise unreasonable raise and provide a chance to win money in a situation where folding – which eliminates any prospect of claiming the pot – cannot.

But any player whose default tendency is to call runs afoul of one of poker's prime strategic precepts: be selective but be aggressive.

The need to be selective is almost self-evident. The player who gets involved in too many hands will win his share of pots and then some, but the goal of poker is to win money, not pots. Playing too many hands is a sure-fire way to go broke.

Aggressive play is important for two reasons. It gets more money into the pot when you have the best hand and are favoured to win, and it provides a second path to victory, whereas passive play provides but one.

Betting and raising are hallmarks of aggressive play that can allow a player to capture the pot and win more money with good hands. Aggressive play can also help a player win some pots simply because his opponent chooses not to call his bet. The passive player, the one who calls but seldom raises, can only win by showing down the best hand. Aggressive play can encourage an opponent to fold a hand that on subsequent betting rounds might improve enough to capture the pot. But passive play removes that tactical ploy from a player's arsenal.

The 'be selective but be aggressive' mantra suggests that unless there's some overriding reason to call, a better course of action might be to either fold or to raise.

Folding takes a player out of situations where he is unsure about how his hand stacks up against an opponent. In uncertain situations, a player is likely to win the minimum when he has the best hand, but lose the maximum when it turns out he is up against an opponent who has a more powerful hand and knows it, and who can bet or raise without fear.

Raising always has the advantage of putting your opponent to the test. The question he'll have to answer is this: am I facing a better hand? Any time you can force your opponent to make a decision, there's a chance he'll decide incorrectly. This allows a selective and aggressive player to win when his opponent folds a better hand, and win more money when he himself holds the best hand.

If you're going to have a default mechanism built into your poker programming, instead of tending to call, let it be this: raise more than you call and fold more than you raise.

There are times when calling is the best course of action, and they're fairly obvious:

✓ Call when you have a drawing hand and need to make your hand as inexpensively as possible.

✓ Call when you want to deceive your opponent into thinking he has a better hand so that he will come out betting on a more costly wagering round and you can check-raise him.

✓ Call when you can take a free card that might improve your hand.

✓ Call from the big blind when no one has raised and you don't have a hand to raise with either.

✓ Call when an opponent to your right comes out betting, you have a huge hand, but by calling instead of raising you believe you'll be able to attract a few additional calls from players who act after you do.

Most other times, you are better off raising or folding.

Tip 18

A Bet Saved Equals a Bet Won

It's no secret that we poker players are an aggressive lot. We like to play. We want to win. We are eager. Given a chance to play a poker hand, most of us will leap to the challenge. The good news is that most poker players seldom let opportunity pass them by. The bad news is that we frequently play too many hands, and play far too deeply into many of the hands we play.

Someone once said, 'Poker is a game of money played with cards.' And it's true. Poker is all about money. The cards are only an incidental means to an end.

What most poker players fail to realize is that a bet saved is equal to a bet won. The money you save by sitting out pots with cards that are better off folded than played, spends just as well as the money you win when you have the best hand or can induce your opponents to fold their hands.

Far too many poker players go full tilt in an attempt to play and win as many pots as they can. This results in playing far too many hands than can be justified by the cards you've been dealt and the willingness of your opponents to call rather than fold.

When you confront players who call more than they should, your bluffs will work far less often than they should – if successful bluffing could be predicated on the strength of an opponent's hand. Because your opponents will call with far too many hands, you won't be able to bluff successfully with as many of your hands as you'd otherwise like. On the other hand, it allows you to bet your good hands for their intrinsic value while counting on your opponents to pay you off with money that they'd be better off saving by folding.

The implications of players failing to save bets by involving themselves in too many hands are far reaching. If you refrain from bluffing because your opponents have shown a marked propensity to call, you will save money. The money you save is going to end up in your pocket at the end of the day, just as surely as the money you manage to win when you bet your hand for value and are called by other players.

It's not glamorous, not by a long shot. Running a spine-tingling, breath-holding, nerve-rattling, pulse-raising bluff feels a lot better than saving a bet by folding, and it's much more fun when you can finally exhale after your last opponent folded and you're able to rake in the pot. But at the end of the day, the money you save is just as valuable – and spends just as well – as money you win.

Playing poker correctly is a high-wire act where you're working without a net. There's a fine line between betting and playing aggressively in order to ensure that you maximize your wins with the best hand, and the need to present as small a target as possible to your opponents. Walking the high wire also requires deft play to save money when you don't have the best hand, in order to ensure that you keep your losses to a minimum.

Tip 19

Folding Before the Flop

What's the most common action you should take at the poker table? It's not flashy, it's not memorable, but it is poker's basic bread and butter play, and good players do it more often than they do anything else – they fold.

Good players, and not-so-good ones too, fold most of the time. The single biggest mistake made by most poker players is that they call when they should have folded. Many players get involved in pots with weak, unplayable starting hands, even seeing the flop with any ace in their hand, regardless of their position in the betting order, with no consideration for the number of opponents in the pot or the amount of betting and raising that has taken place before it is their turn to act.

Many players will *cold-call* a raise, voluntarily investing two bets in a hand they should fold. A much stronger hand is needed to call a raise than to do the raising yourself. Calling a raise requires a hand that figures to be better than the one held by the guy doing the raising – so be sure of your position before you risk it.

I've held many a hand that I was preparing to raise with, only to have an opponent snatch the rug right out from under my feet by raising before the action got around to me. Much of the time that hand I was considering raising with is no longer even a calling hand and winds up in the muck. Hands such as A-J, A-T, K-J, K-T, Q-J and J-T all fall into this category. So do those ace-anything hands you'd raise with from the button or even next to it, if no one had voluntarily entered the pot before it was your turn to act.

When their initiative is filched from right under their noses, many players become irritated and agitated. Their stubbornness costs them money when they refuse to get away from a good hand, even when all the signs are indicating that the opponent's hand is better. You see it all the time, an angry slam-down of a hand like A-T because another player raised before they could act.

Players who react like this have got it backwards. Instead of being upset, they ought to be thankful. Their opponent's raise probably saved them money and they should be relieved – even thankful – instead of angry. After all, money saved spends just as well as money won, and any time I can get a free pass out of a pot knowing my hand is probably a long shot that won't be offset by the pot odds, I'm happy.

When you are faced with a raise, the hand you're holding quickly changes categories. Most likely it becomes a folding hand. Sometimes it's a big hand and you ought to re-raise with it. But it's seldom a calling hand. If I'm in the *cutoff* seat – the seat to the immediate right of the button – or on the button, and someone raises in front of me, I'm going to throw away many of the hands that I would have raised with, had no one entered the pot before the action reached me.

On the other hand, if I'm holding a big pair, I'm going to make it three-bets in hopes of playing heads-up against the initial raiser. When that happens I have a big advantage going into the flop. Not only did I get the last raise in, but I'll have position on my opponent throughout the entire hand.

That doesn't guarantee I'm going to play that hand down to the river. If I made it three bets with J-J and the flop contained an ace and a king, I'd be a fool to keep playing if there were any appreciable action. But if no overcards fall, I'm a favourite over anyone who would raise with a pair of nines through a pair of aces, as well as A-K, A-Q, A-J and K-Q.

Take a look at that last sentence. You're probably thinking, 'This guy's nuts. In what world is his pair of jacks favourite over a pair of aces?' In the poker world, of course. And here's why. Although J-J is certainly not a favourite if my opponent has a pair of aces, kings or queens, that pair of jacks is favoured over the range of his raising hands. If my opponent will raise with any hand ranging from a pair of nines through a pair of aces, as well as A-K, A-Q, A-J and K-Q, here's how the arithmetic works out:

There are six ways to make any pair and 16 ways to combine two cards, such as A-K or K-Q. If my opponent will raise with 9-9 through A-A, that's five pairs or 30 different combinations, plus an additional combination that comprises the two remaining jacks. Remember, I have two jacks in my hand, so only two jacks remain unaccounted for in this deck.

He'll also raise with A-K, A-Q, A-J and K-Q. With 16 ways to make each of those combinations, minus eight combinations due to my holding two jacks, that's another 56 hands he will raise with, for a total of 87 hands – 56 big card combinations plus 31 combinations of cards that form a pair.

At this point that pair of jacks in my hand is ahead of all but 18 of these 87 combinations – six ways each to form a pair of queens, kings and aces – and tied with an opponent who might have been dealt the remaining two jacks. So my jacks are a favourite when compared to the possible hands my opponent holds.

The lessons of a bet saved equalling a bet won and raising more than you call while folding more than you raise all come into play here. Like so many of these tips they are interrelated and intertwined, and they comprise an overall strategic approach towards winning poker.

Tip 20

Folding After the Flop

Most of your folds will be relatively simple decisions that are made before investing in the flop. However, sometimes you'll see the flop, or even the turn and river before confronting a decision about folding or continuing to play. The longer you're involved in a hand, the more difficult it is to fold. Often the size of the pot is big enough to make drawing correct, even when your chances of winning appear slim. The opposite can be true too. If you've flopped a straight draw against only one opponent in a hold'em game, chances are you will not have the right odds to keep calling.

Sometimes you'll find out via the betting and raising that you are not the favourite even when you hold what is usually a good hand. You might have been the aggressor before the flop with A-K, been fortunate enough to see an ace hit the board, and yet watch with shocked indignation when there's a bet, a call and a raise before it's your turn to act.

Top pair, even with the best possible kicker, probably isn't any good at this point, particularly if the board contains three cards of the same suit or an obvious straight draw. Even when no flush is possible, one of your opponents might have made a set and is a big favourite. You can keep calling – your opponents will love you for it if you do – or you can do the smart thing and save your money for a better situation.

Sometimes it's easy to fold, but other decisions are strictly judgment calls based on how well you read your opponents and your analysis of the betting and raising that's transpired before the action gets around to you. Experience helps. So does your willingness to see things as they really are, and not play poker with a denial mindset that allows you to talk yourself into calling with top pair because some part of your brain wants to believe that your opponent really did not make a flush and your hand – top pair with top kicker – is still good despite overwhelming evidence to the contrary.

The fact that the odds are always shifting about in poker, and that you don't have to play a hand to its conclusion just because you called a bet or two on earlier rounds, is what enables good players to win at poker. You don't have this option in most casino games. You make a bet at a table game and for the most part that bet is still working until the particular confrontation you wagered on has ended. And even when a surrender option is available, the house has the best of the deal.

Poker is different. You always have the ability to opt in and opt out. And it's often the ability and willingness to fold your tent and steal away into the night – saved money clutched tightly in your hot little hands – that provides the resources for you to play another hand when you do have the best of it.

I know you came to play. And getting involved in a hand and slugging it out with the guys and gals at the table is a lot more fun than sitting on the sidelines. But folding is what you have to do most of the time in order to be a winning player.

Watch the good players. They play far fewer hands than you do. If you don't believe me, just look and see for yourself. It only seems like they're always in there slugging because they play very aggressively whenever they do enter a pot, and that's what you remember. But the one play they make above all others is the simplest and most boring in poker. They fold – before the flop and after it too.

Tip 21

Play Your Best Game

At the risk of belabouring the obvious, here's one of those willpower tips that some players seem to be able to master in the wink of an eye and others will have difficulty with all of their lives. Play your best – always. While this admonition seems simple and obvious, few of us always play our best – and here's why.

Poker is too much fun

It's so much fun, in fact, that we'd much rather play a hand than fold it. We get caught up in playing far too many hands, and we do it simply because it's fun.

We call too much

Most players enter far too many pots and refrain from folding when their promising holdings are not caressed by the flop. They then compound this faux pas by failing to raise in situations that clearly call for it. Suppose you hold K-J in an unraised pot. The flop is K-8-4 of mixed suits and the big blind comes out betting. This is an almost automatic raising situation.

Why? Because, you might have the best hand right now, and you certainly don't want someone who entered the pot in late position with a hand like 8-7 or 7-6 to take a card off the deck and beat you. Even if you knew your opponent held a king with a better kicker, once you decide to play, you are better off raising than calling. If you had a 25 per cent chance of winning the pot against three or four opponents, but were able to drive out two or three opponents by raising, you might improve your own chances of winning to 40 per cent. While you're still an underdog, raising increases your chances of winning – never mind all the dead money left in the pot by those players your raise manages to eliminate.

We tend to play to the level of our competition

I'll bet that if you found yourself in a game with the last eight winners of the World Series of Poker, or even with the eight best players in your local cardroom, you'd play better than you usually do because you'd have a lot more respect for your opponents. But if you were in a game with eight terrible players, you might find yourself playing the same wretched brand of poker they do. Poker can be a seductive game that often leads us down a primrose path, where we find ourselves playing just like our opponents – even when we should know better.

Don't play when you're psychologically weakened

Poker is tough enough to beat when you're at your best. If you're tired, stressed out, dealing with personal issues, or you've got the blues, don't play. One of the real benefits of playing online or in traditional casinos is that the game never really ends. It will be there whenever you are. Don't make the fatal mistake of taking your troubles out on your bankroll.

Playing less than your best is no reason to despair, and certainly not a reason for simply repeating the mistakes you made in the past. If that metaphorical journey of one thousand miles does begin with the first step, take that step now. But remember, in poker, as in life itself, talk comes cheaply. Achieving most goals takes unrelenting effort, but playing your best takes nothing more than simple willpower.

Tip 22   Resolutions to Keep You Playing Your Best

You can make poker resolutions any time, it doesn't have to be New Year's Eve. Here are some resolutions I made a number of years ago and you're cordially invited to consider them your own if you believe that adopting them will help to improve your game. There are only four, but they cover a lot of ground.

Learn another game

With its relentless television coverage, hold'em has become the game of choice for most poker players. In fact, I wouldn't be surprised if some players have never played another form of poker in their lives.

There are good reasons to learn other games. Sometimes the waiting list for a hold'em game might be crowded. Sometimes the line-up at the hold'em game is tougher than it is at other tables. And mixed games, in which players have a go at alternating rounds of hold'em and other games such as Omaha, razz, seven-card stud or triple-draw lowball, are growing in popularity. You can't hope to win a mixed game tournament or beat a cash game without playing all of these games at a high level of competence.

Never go on tilt, never play less than your best

Controlling emotions in the heat of battle is a never-ending battle players have to fight with themselves. With senses rubbed raw by a bad beat administered by a particularly obnoxious player, you might have to get up and walk away from the table until you've finished devouring your own innards.

When I'm not at my best, I usually go to the movies instead of continuing to play. After all, popcorn is still cheap whether you're on top of your game or not.

Narrow the target

You can't present your opponents with a big target to shoot at and expect to win very much money. Narrowing the target is another way of saying that you won't win if you take the worst of it by risking too much money in unfavourable situations.

You can't play hunches if you hope to present a narrow target. You can't cold-call raises willy-nilly because you hope a miracle card will turn up. You can't play marginal starting cards in early position, and you can't go on proving what a tough, tricky player you are by attempting to bluff players who call too often.

You will always earn more money in a poker game by virtue of your opponents' mistakes than your own strokes of genius. It takes great skill along with a good bit of luck to manoeuvre a decent player into making a serious error in judgment. It takes nothing more than basic technique to gather in all those extra bets that come from players who called when they really should have folded.

The point of narrowing the target is that there's no need to give your opponents a handicap and then have to rise to extraordinary heights to beat them, when good play will garner the laurels.

Model successful behaviour and play

I've never thrown cards, insulted a dealer, or otherwise made a fool of myself in a casino or public cardroom. This is not, after all, life and death. It's just a game.

I have always resolved to model my own behaviour, deportment and playing style after players I admire – and to continue learning from them. The players I admire are wholly professional in their approach to the game. They carry themselves as well as they play, and they are winning players over the course of their careers. I learn by watching their play, reading their books, talking to them, and attempting to discern the secrets of their success in the hope that they rub off on me.

The truth is deceptively simple: if you're not ready to play your best, don't play. And when you do play, keep your own standards foremost in your mind. Don't tumble down to the level of your opponents. Tell yourself it's okay to play your best, then do it.

Tip 23

Where Does the Money Come From?

Most of the money you win at poker comes from opponents' mistakes rather than your own poker skills – transcendent though they may be. It stands to reason that not all poker games are created equally, and finding the best game – and the best seat in the game you choose – is worth at least some time and effort to uncover.

If you live in an area where the local card room is small, you won't have much of a choice when it comes to selecting the best game. You might have to play below or above your preferred betting limits if you want to play in the best available game. You might not even have a choice of games. The best game might be the only game, and your only choice is to take it or leave it. But even when there is only one game available to you, be sure to change seats whenever it positions you on the proper side of overly cautious, overly aggressive or very strong players.

You will find myriad games online. At wagering limits of $5–$10 and lower and no-limit games of $2–$4 and below, you will have a choice of games at many online cardrooms. At some of the bigger online rooms, you'll find a choice of games at higher betting limits too, if that's what you want.

To demonstrate the critical importance of game selection I used commercial poker simulation software to simulate 50 years of poker. The first time I ran this simulation I placed identical player profiles in each seat, and the big winner raked in 60 cents per hour – a figure attributable to luck – because each player profile was programmed to make the same decisions under identical conditions. When I substituted one player who played very few hands and another who played too many, the big winner's profits increased twenty-fold, to $12 per hour.

The message here is that it doesn't take too many poor players to turn what was a virtually unbeatable game into one in which all but the two poor players came away from as lifetime winners.

You want aggressive, tough and talented players – as well as maniacs, who raise far too frequently regardless of whether they have a hand or not – on your right. They will act before you and you can step out of the way of their agressive raises if you don't have a strong hand, but re-raise them whenever you have a hand. That way, you avoid costly confrontations you are unlikely to win, and you get more money in the pot when you have a hand that is likely to be the winner.

Passive players belong on your left, because you can manipulate them into and out of the pot by virtue of your bets and raises.

Although you won't always be able to get your opponents perfectly positioned, you can continue to look for the best seat at the table, and move into it whenever it becomes available.

If a variety of games are available, look over the other games periodically to be sure yours is still the best. You're looking for the party table. Happy, jovial players busily interacting with each other and not paying too much attention to what's going on in the game frequently make the best opponents. If they have a lot of chips in front of them, that's even better.

While a lot of chips might mean a player is currently winning, it might also mean he's come to gamble. And you can easily tell the difference. Frequent calling, lots of banter, flirting, joking and table-talk are the marks of casual recreational players. They're out to have a good time, and you should position yourself at their table. Once you're in the right game at the right table, choose your seat carefully. Players who are tight, timid and easy to bluff belong on your left, while loose, skilful, aggressive players, as well as those with lots of chips, belong on your right.

Tip 24

The Front-loaded Effect

Compared to many other forms of poker, Texas hold'em is a front-loaded game. Most of the time your hand will be formed on the flop because five of the seven cards that you'll use to make your best poker hand will be in play at that point.

Not only do you get to see five-sevenths – or 71 per cent – of your hand on the flop, but the price is only one round of betting, which makes this a relative bargain. The flip side of the equation is that there are three remaining betting rounds but only two cards to come that can be used to complete your hand.

The implications of hold'em's front-loaded nature cannot be overlooked. Because 71 per cent of your hand is formed by the time you see the flop, and you receive the majority of your hand for the bargain price of one bet, it makes the rest of the hand expensive by comparison. As a result, you should consider abandoning your quest for the pot unless you've had a big hand to begin with – one that can survive the flop without any help – or the flop helps you by pairing one or both of your big cards, or provides you with a draw to a straight or a flush.

In fact, if you need to adopt a default position, just release any hand that cannot survive the flop on its own and is not helped by the flop – unless there is some other compelling reason to keep playing.

The relationship between the cost of the flop and the fact that you will receive five-sevenths of your hand for that price, especially when compared against the high cost of paying for the remaining 29 per cent of your hand, makes hold'em the front-loaded game that it is.

One of the hallmarks of poor play is unwillingness on the part of many players to release a hand on the flop. They stick around on a hunch and some hope, neither of which grace them often enough to make investing in hopeful hands worthwhile in the long run. It's not that drawing a card is such a bad strategic decision in itself.

The bad decision is drawing a card at a price that's not offset by the reward if you get lucky.

In other words, the odds against improving your hand when you go from the flop to the turn and from the turn to the river generally make buying another card a poor decision. The exception to this is when the flop presents you with a good flush draw or a good straight draw and you have a sufficient number of opponents to ensure that the size of the pot you're hoping to win more than offsets the odds against completing you hand.

The relationship between the size of the pot and the odds against completing your hand exists aside and apart from the front-loaded nature of hold'em. It is always present regardless of the form of poker you're playing. But the fact that you get to see the majority of your cards early, and for a bargain price too, makes the decision to fold or continue on after you've seen the flop of critical importance.

If you think this concept is important in fixed-limit hold'em, wait until you consider pot-limit and no-limit hold'em games. In those games, especially when you and your opponent each have a deep stack of chips, a decision on the flop is critical. Big-bet poker is frequently a game of implied odds. If you can see the flop inexpensively and catch a big hand in the process, you stand a good chance of winning each and every one of your opponent's chips in the process.

But your opponent has a chance of taking all your chips too, which makes big bet poker more of a trapping, cat-and-mouse game than fixed-limit poker, where you are really pressing small edges by betting and raising as often as possible.

If you can see 71 per cent of your hand for an inexpensive price and your opponent flops a good hand while you flop a great one, you can take his entire stack in one sweet front-loaded stroke.

If you think about the front-loaded nature of Texas hold'em the implications will become more and more apparent. But the most important implication is that it can be very costly to play beyond the flop. Because the best hold'em hand on the flop is generally the best hand on the river, you'll find yourself releasing most of the hands that haven't panned out once you see the flop.

Tip 25

Classify and Categorize Your Opponents

As you gain more experience playing poker you'll notice that many of your opponents often play as though they were on autopilot. They look at their hand, decide whether to play or not, and then go on with whatever else they might have been doing. And 'whatever else' can include anything from watching a ball game on TV to chatting with other players or reading the morning newspaper.

All too frequently 'whatever else' does not include studying their opponents, categorizing their play, and making mental notes they can draw on later. Online players have an even better option at their disposal. They can take notes about an opponent right on their computer, and these notes will pop up any time this particular opponent ventures into their game. Even if it's an opponent they haven't seen in months, they'll have notes at their disposal.

But far too many online players succumb to other distractions, from watching TV or reading while they play, to playing so many games simultaneously that they have no time to take notes on their opponents' tendencies.

The choice is yours. You can either pay attention to other players in your game or not. But if you do, your game will be better for it.

While most players concentrate on their adversaries whenever they are involved in a hand, the best time to study other players at the table is when you are not encumbered by having to make decisions about a hand you're playing. In other words, the best time to study opponents is when you are not involved in a hand.

If you've never done this before and are at a loss for how best to go about it, here are a few suggestions that might prove useful to you.

Categorize your opponents' play

Poker players are fond of describing players as loose or tight, but that's not enough. You really need to set up a matrix that looks something like this:

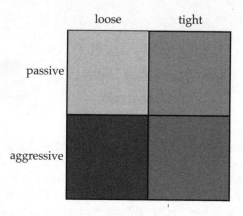

This allows you to categorize opponents into one of four archetypes: loose-passive, loose-aggressive, tight-passive and tight-aggressive.

This simple player profiling provides you with a substantial amount of tactical options during a game.

For example, against an opponent who is loose-passive, you should refrain from bluffing, because he will call too frequently to make bluffing profitable. Instead, you can bet your good hands for value, secure in the knowledge that he will call you when he has weaker hands.

If your opponent is tight-passive, bluff whenever you get a chance. He tends to fold too much and is also reluctant to raise with anything but the very best hands.

When your opponent is loose-aggressive, you want to sit to his left, so you can act after he does and raise or re-raise when you have a good hand.

If you are up against a tight-aggressive player, you'll need to be wary. They play well, and that's the very playing style you should aspire to.

Watch for betting patterns. If you pay attention to betting patterns and then see the hands that players turn up at the showdown, you'll get a very good idea about the various playing styles of your opponents. If you are playing online you should make notes about playing styles when not involved in a hand, and use that information whenever you need to make a borderline decision based on the nature of your opponent's playing style as much as on the nature of the cards you hold.

There's no special skill required to do this. All that's needed are basic powers of observation along with a desire to take advantage of your downtime to gather as much information as you can about how your opponents play.

Information just seems to float above the poker table, and it's there for anyone to take advantage of. Far too many players are easily distracted and find themselves caught up in pursuits that may be enjoyable but won't do anything to increases their chances of winning. You'll be a far better player for taking advantage of opportunities that present themselves to you any time you're not involved in a hand.

Tip 26

Playing the Odds

Doing arithmetic and playing poker at the same time is difficult for most of us. If you commit the Odds and Outs chart to memory, you will be spared this drudgery. If memorizing a chart is not your thing, don't worry; there's another way to put the odds in your favour. Just multiply your outs – which is what poker players call cards that will complete your hand – by two, add two to that sum, and you'll have a rough approximation of the chance that you'll make your hand.

Suppose you have a flush draw on the turn. You have nine outs. Nine times two equals 18, and 18 plus two equals 20. That's pretty close to the 19.6 per cent chance of making your flush that you'd come up with if you worked out the answer mathematically.

But committing this chart to memory is easy, and when you do, you'll never have to figure a thing. Just tap your memory banks for the correct figure.

The chart on page 82 shows the chance of making your hand, expressed as a percentage, and the odds against making it with two cards to come – the turn and the river – and with one card remaining – the river.

Odds and percentages are two different ways of looking at the same thing. Odds give you the bad news first and are a ratio of failures to successes. The first number gives the predicted failures and the second number represents expected successes. When you ask, 'What are the odds?,' you are really asking, 'What is the expected ratio of failures to successes?' If the odds against your horse winning a race are 7-to-2 it means that if this race were to be run nine times – 7 + 2 = 9 – your horse figures to lose seven of those races and win two.

A percentage in this chart represents the chances of a given hand being completed. If you flop a flush draw, you can expect to complete it either on the turn or on the river 35 times out of 100.

Outs Common Draw	Flop to the River		Turn to the River	
	Per cent	Odds	Per cent	Odds
20	67.5	0.48-to-1	43.5	1.30-to-1
19	65.0	0.54-to-1	41.3	1.42-to-1
18	62.4	0.60-to-1	39.1	1.56-to-1
17	59.8	0.67-to-1	37.0	1.71-to-1
16	57.0	0.75-to-1	34.8	1.88-to-1
15 Straight + Flush	54.1	0.85-to-1	32.6	2.07-to-1
14	51.2	0.95-to-1	30.4	2.29-to-1
13	48.1	1.08-to-1	28.3	2.54-to-1
12	45.0	1.22-to-1	26.1	2.83-to-1
11	41.7	1.40-to-1	23.9	3.18-to-1
10	38.4	1.60-to-1	21.7	3.60-to-1
9 Flush	35.0	1.86-to-1	19.6	4.11-to-1
8 Straight	31.5	2.17-to-1	17.4	4.75-to-1
7	27.8	2.60-to-1	15.2	5.57-to-1
6	24.1	3.15-to-1	13.0	6.67-to-1
5	20.3	3.93-to-1	10.9	8.20-to-1
4 Pair or Inside Straight Draw	16.5	5.06-to-1	8.7	10.50-to-1
3	12.5	7.00-to-1	6.5	14.33-to-1
2	8.4	10.90-to-1	4.3	22.00-to-1
1	4.3	22.26-to-1	2.2	45.00-to-1

Other Probabilities

A wired pair flops a set nearly 12 per cent of the time

If you are dealt A-K, you'll flop at least one ace or king 32.4 per cent

Two suited cards will make a flush 6.5 per cent

Two suited cards flops a flush 0.8 per cent

Two suited cards flops a four flush 10.9 per cent

Two unmatched cards will make a split pair 2.2 per cent

Here's how you can put this to use. If you have only a 20 per cent chance of winning, the cost of your call should not be more than 20 per cent of the pot's total. With a 32 per cent chance, you can call a bet up to one-third the size of the pot. If your chances of winning are only ten per cent, don't call any bet that's more than ten per cent of the pot's size.

Hanging on to unprofitable draws for whatever reason – and many players persist in drawing to long shots even when they really do know better – can be a major leak in one's game. For many it's the sole reason they are lifelong losing players instead of lifelong winners.

There's no real excuse for that kind of play, even if you are not mathematically inclined – and if you're in this category, you're in the majority. You don't have to do arithmetic at the poker table, because it's all been worked out for you in advance. Just count the size of the pot, or even approximate it, and compare the relationship of the size of the pot to the bet you have to call. This will give you the pot odds. Then compare that to the odds against making your hand. If the pot is $60 and you had to call a ten-dollar bet, the pot is offering 6-to-1 odds. If you have a flush draw, the odds against completing it are only 1.86-to-1. Because the pot odds exceed the odds against making your hand, it pays to call this bet in the long run. It's that easy.

Tip 27

Follow the Money

What's the number one mistake made by most poker players? They call too often in situations when they should fold. Nothing else is even close. This is by far the single biggest mistake you'll see at the poker table.

Poker players frequently make other mistakes too. They call instead of raise, fold when they should raise, raise when folding is the best course of action, check when they ought to bet, and bet when checking should be their choice.

But day in and day out, at all levels and all limits, players call too frequently. Mistake Number One is this, and we'll repeat it again: players call when they should fold.

Players call too much because poker is fun. Most players are recreational players. They come to play, and whether it's online or at a traditional casino, they just want to get in there and play hands. Folding all the time is no fun at all.

Nobody likes folding hand after hand, but if your goal is to win money at the poker table, that's usually what you'll have to do. You might not have as much fun as your opponents – not until you walk out of the casino with a lot of chips and they are left with a pocket full of hope and not much else.

Now that you know that most players call much more than they ought to and fold far too infrequently, you can take advantage of these tendencies.

When a player will call too often and fold too infrequently, he will not be easy to bluff. But you can get him to call with a weak hand that he would check if the choice were his. Save your bluffs for good, strong players and bet your marginal hands for value against players who call all the time. Weak opponents are the type who will call with a lesser hand than yours.

In a tournament or a no-limit cash game you might not want to play as many marginal hands. But when you do make a big hand, you can nickel and dime your adversary into calling his money away – particularly if you're able to price him into the pot by betting just enough to seduce him into calling with a losing hand. Once you reach the turn or the river, you can put him all-in for his remaining money, and now, because the pot has grown so large, he's very likely to call himself right out of the tournament.

In a limit game, you don't have to be wary of betting the river if you bet the turn and were not raised. Unless the river card makes an obvious flush or straight for an opponent, chances are good that your hand is still the strongest one in play. Because hold'em is such a front-loaded game, hands that are good on the flop and the turn tend to be good on the river too.

This is a compelling argument for driving most of your good hands by betting and raising as long as cards that appear to help opponents – such as cards that complete obvious draws – don't show up on the turn or river.

Tip 28

Record Keeping

Without accurate records, you'll never know how good a player you are. If you are serious about poker you have to treat your game as a business or a profession. Every business keeps records. Without them, a business owner has no idea of what it costs to make, sell or inventory their product, and no way of knowing whether their bottom line will be written in black or red.

In hold'em, as in every form of poker, you need to be concerned about two basic statistical parameters: your *win rate*, which is the average amount of money won or lost per hour or per hundred hands; and the *standard deviation*, which measures those short-term fluctuations we all call 'luck.'

Next time you play poker take a small note pad and pencil with you and record the amount of your buy-in. Then record the following information each hour:

✓ Amount won or lost during that hour.

✓ The game you're playing in (e.g. $2–$4 hold'em).

✓ Total hours played that session, or the number of hands if you're playing online. Because so many more hands are dealt per hour online, you can equate 100 online hands to three hours of regular casino poker.

When you get home, you'll also want to record this cumulative information:

✓ The amount won or lost for the entire year to date.

✓ The total number of hours or hands played during the current year.

Computing your win or loss rate is simple. Divide the amount of money won or lost by the number of hours or hands played. This shows the average amount won or lost per hour or per hundred hands played.

Knowing how much you are winning or losing is important. But it is equally important to know whether that average, or mean, is an accurate indicator of the data it represents.

In poker, two players might each win an average of $15 per hour. But one might experience big wins and big losses very infrequently, while the other often experiences substantial fluctuations to arrive at the same average winnings. The player who can achieve that win rate while putting less of his or her money at risk is generally better off.

That's where the standard deviation comes into play, and you can calculate it by hand, on most pocket calculators, or on any computer spreadsheet program.

Maximizing your hourly winnings while minimizing your standard deviation is a real conundrum. If you choose to take the risks required to maximize winnings, such as getting all those extra bets in whenever you believe you have the best of it, you tend to increase bankroll fluctuations because you're not going to come out on top in every one of those marginal situations.

If calculating your standard deviation still seems burdensome, here's a shortcut. Calculate it for 100 hours play. Then do the same thing a few months later. See if you've been able to reduce your standard deviation while increasing or at least maintaining your win rate. If you're able to do this, you've reduced the amount of money you're risking. The gamble, in essence, has got better.

From a statistical viewpoint, when you live on the edge you are flying in the face of minimizing your standard deviation. Because of this, you must come to terms with your own risk tolerance and how much of your bankroll you're willing to risk in order to gain these marginal boosts in earnings. If you're not comfortable at a certain level of risk, or playing on a short bankroll, you'd be better off concentrating on minimizing your standard deviation rather than maximizing your winnings.

You can play on a shorter bankroll by avoiding marginal situations that require you to put additional money into the pot when it's a close call. If you're a winning player, you'll eventually win just as much money. It will just take more hours at the table to reach your goals.

Tip 29

Playing with Maniacs

Loose, aggressive games generate the most action, but they can be frustrating too. A gaggle of players in each pot means more money when you win, but so often someone who shouldn't be in the pot seems to catch a miraculous card and beats you. Sometimes there's a maniac in the game too. He's the kind of player who raises almost all the time, regardless of whether he has a hand or not. But you can win a lot in these games too, because there's more money in play on every hand, and that money has got to go somewhere, so why not win some for yourself?

Here are some tips for playing well and retaining your sanity in extremely loose, aggressive, no-fold'em hold'em games.

Expect big swings

You'll experience unavoidably big swings in your bankroll. More players per pot means increased chances that good hands will be run down by lesser ones. But that's offset because the pots you win will be larger. While your win rate in these games should be more than it would be in tighter games, the standard deviation – that statistical measure of variability – will be much higher. Because of this, many players believe they are doing worse in these games when they are simply looking at a geometrical increase in the game's short-term variance. In the long run, you ought to make more money in loose games, providing of course you have a bankroll that can withstand bigger fluctuations.

If you can't live with that degree of instability, or if your bankroll won't sustain extreme fluctuations, you'll have to seek out games that are not as loose and not as aggressive.

Starting hands change in value

In loose, aggressive games certain starting hands increase in value while others fall. Suited connectors have more potential because you'll probably rake in a big pot when they win. Miss the flop and you can easily release these hands.

Big, unsuited cards go down in value. Hands such as A-10, A-J and Q-K do not play well against a big, aggressive field. With hands like these you have to limit the field if you play them at all.

Sit to the maniac's left
When you're in a game with a maniac, position yourself to his left – you want to act after he does. That enables you to re-raise when you have a good hand. When you are able to do this, you stand a good chance of playing your good hand heads-up against his hand, which figures to be a lot weaker than yours.

Don't call if you can't raise. From an early position in a loose, aggressive game don't call with a hand that you wouldn't ordinarily raise with. One of the worst feelings imaginable is to find yourself trapped for two or three bets in loose, aggressive games with hands that may be worth a call but not a raise. When you're playing in a game where the majority of pots are raised, you simply cannot afford to play bargain hands like 9-8 suited from early position. Hands like these are only worth playing if you can see the flop for one bet. When the cost of these highly speculative hands is two bets – or sometimes three – it is unlikely that the money in the pot will ever exceed the odds against making your hand.

If you can stand life on the edge, if big swings can be absorbed by your bankroll, and if you are comfortable with a high level of risk, you'll do well in loose, aggressive games. If it's the only game in town and you feel compelled to play in spite of yourself, be sure to restrict the hands you play from an early position and be willing to re-raise whenever you need to thin out the field.

Tip 30

What's Important

Whether you read this or any other book aimed at improving your poker, you'll come across so much information that it's actually difficult to digest it all. Although you'll probably understand each of the concepts presented in this book, it will be difficult if not impossible to remember all of them in the heat of combat.

Poker is not chess. You don't have a lot of time to ponder decisions and weigh each and every piece of information before acting on your hand. You've got a limited amount of time to make decisions at the poker table. You'll eventually put all of the concepts in this book to use at the table, but you can't expect to do it overnight.

This all brings up the obvious question – what should you think about first?

Actually, there are three areas of concern that are of equal importance, and we'll take them one at a time. They are:

✓ Frequent decisions

✓ Costly decisions

✓ Decisions influencing subsequent actions

Frequent decisions:

If you make a mistake with decisions that occur frequently, such as deciding whether to call the blind or how you go about selecting your starting hands, errors can be costly even though each individual error may not be costly in itself. But if you make the same error over and over again, the cost of that mistake adds up quickly. Because each individual error may go unnoticed, the sum of those small mistakes can amount to a big leak in your game. And because an error may go unnoticed, it can have a pernicious effect.

That's why it's so critically important to learn the rudiments of the game and know them cold. Things that recur in poker must be handled correctly, and good players handle them correctly all of the time. Knowing the basics and knowing them cold goes a long way to removing repetitive errors from your game.

Costly decisions

Costly decisions are important for obvious reasons, even if they do not occur as regularly as basic, repetitive, frequent decisions. If you're facing a $10 bet on the river into a $90 pot and you think there's a 70 per cent chance you're beaten, what should you do? A wrong decision can be a costly error. If you call that last bet and you lose, which will happen the majority of the time, you'll cost yourself one additional bet. But if you fold a hand that would have won, the cost is nine bets, and that's a lot higher.

Actually, if you estimate you have a 70 per cent chance of losing, it means you have a 30 per cent chance of winning. If you could replay this hand 1,000 times, you'd lose $10 for every 700 times you play at a loss of $7,000. However, you'd win the entire $90 pot on 300 occasions, which amounts to a win of $27,000. If you subtract your losses from your wins, you'd walk away with a net profit of $20,000. If you divide that $20,000 by the 1,000 hands it would take you to win it, you'll find that each correct decision is worth $20 to you.

Decisions influencing subsequent actions

A bad decision made late in a hand is usually not as consequential as making one early. That's because in poker, as in so much of life, early decisions lead you to related decisions that occur subsequently.

If you get involved early with a hand that screams out, 'I should have known better,' you'll often find yourself tied to a hand that catches a piece of the flop – not enough of a hand to bet aggressively but seductive enough to keep you calling. When that happens you have a hand that is likely to win a small pot or lose a big one.

This is simply not what you want to do in most poker games. You are usually better off avoiding dicey hands that can hurt you a lot more than help you. However, it's tougher to extricate yourself from these situations in a live game than it is to discuss them as pieces of poker theory.

Do yourself a big favour. While you're working diligently to raise your game, pay close attention to these three areas of concern and just watch your results improve.

Tip 31

Three Ways to Play Winning Hold'em

Here are some ways to jump-start your hold'em game. Even if these concepts are familiar to you, they're worth reviewing again just to be sure you still have a firm hand on the plough.

Play few hands from early position

There's an old adage that the three most important factors in a real estate decision are: location, location, location. It translates to poker pretty nicely because the three most important considerations in choosing a hand to play are: position, position, position.

Position in the betting order is so important that certain hands which should be folded early in the betting order – before you have the benefit of seeing how many opponents will enter the pot and whether they will come in calling or raising – are hands you can raise with when you act late in the hand.

When you play hold'em correctly, you won't find yourself playing many hands from early position unless you experience a miraculous run of good cards. In fact, if all you take away from this book is an appreciation of the fact that you should player fewer hands but be more aggressive with the hands you do play, you will improve your game significantly.

Why big suited cards are more valuable than unsuited cards of the same rank

Although it's nice to flop a flush when you have big suited cards, it won't happen very often. To be precise about it, you'll flop a flush less than one per cent of the time that you're dealt two suited starting cards.

But you will flop four to a flush nearly 11 per cent of the time. When you do flop four cards to a flush, you'll complete your hand 35 per cent of the time. But it's even better than that. If you flop a four-flush with big cards, you'll probably win if you complete your flush – and as long as your two big cards are bigger than the community cards on the board, you might win by pairing one of your cards too.

In other words, drawing to a flush allows you to stay in the game and gives you a chance to win even if you miss your flush but pair-up one of your big cards in the process. The odds that you'll either complete your flush or pair one of your two hole cards are better than even money. And while that's no guarantee of winning, you're in pretty good shape as long as both of your hole cards are bigger than any of the community cards on the board.

On the other hand, if you didn't flop a four flush, sticking around in the game usually isn't worth it if you're just hoping to pair one of your hole cards.

Smaller suited cards don't offer the same opportunity, because there's less of a chance that your smallish hole cards will be able to win by pairing.

Pushing and pulling
With drawing hands, such as a four-flush and a straight draw that can be completed by any of eight cards, you are in a situation that cries out for a large number of opponents. While the odds are against completing a straight or a flush, they are very powerful hands that figure to win when you make them. A draw to this kind of hand is an 'either / or' situation. You'll either make a very big hand or you'll be left with a hand that probably can't even beat a bluff.

You want a lot of opponents because you figure to beat all of them if you get lucky. You'd love to be paid off when you make your hand. When that's the case, you want to pull them into the pot.

The situation differs when you have a big pair. Generally, they don't grow into very big hands without a lot of luck. Big pairs have a better chance of holding up against fewer opponents.

If you have the biggest pair to begin with, you're heavily favoured against any lesser pairs, and one of your goals in this situation is to push out any hands that might otherwise stick around to outdraw you if the price is right. The way to accomplish this is by betting and raising, or if you're in early position with a good hand and your opponents are aggressive, you can try for a check-raise.

Playing few hands from an early position, understanding the nature of big suited cards, and knowing when to draw players into the pot and when to push them out will take you a long way down the road to improving your game.

Tip 32

Counter-intuitive Strategy

Whether you call it card sense or intuition, there's more to hold'em than knowing the odds and how your opponents play. Poker intuition is like a sixth sense. But a lot of strategy is counter-intuitive too, and here are a few bits and pieces to show you that conventional wisdom, as the song goes, '... ain't necessarily so'.

You often have to bet a weak hand in order to win, but you can frequently afford to check a strong one

Most of the time you bet strong hands and fold weak ones, but not all the time. Suppose you raised before the flop with A-K. Three rags – weak cards – fell and you've got only one or two opponents but no hand. What should you do? Bet. How else are you going to get anyone holding a small pair to credit you with a bigger pair and release his hand? When the turn is also a blank you bet again. Once again both of your opponents call. The river card is a king. Now you've got top pair and the best possible kicker.

You could come out betting, but you were called on the flop and the turn by two opponents. One of them must have something. And if that something is two pair or a set, you'll lose an additional bet by wagering. But here's counter-intuitive strategy at work. You made a legitimate hand, and now you can afford to check. If everyone checks, you'll win the showdown. If your check induces one of your adversaries to bluff, your call will win the pot. This enables you to win a bet you wouldn't have if you came out betting and your opponents released their hands.

That's the best of both worlds. You save a bet whenever an opponent holds a better hand and is planning to raise, and you earn an additional bet if your opponent bluffs in a situation in which he would have folded if you were the bettor.

You don't necessarily want to make the biggest hand

Suppose you're holding A-J. Which of these two flops would you prefer, J-7-4 or A-7-4?

While a pair of aces is certainly bigger than jacks, consider this. With A-J you won't be sure you have the best hand any time an ace flops. And if the pot was raised before the flop, your doubts are quickly magnified.

But J-7-4 yields top pair with the best possible kicker. Concerns about straights and flushes not withstanding, your only worry is a king or queen appearing on the turn or river. If an ace comes up you'll have two pair and be a heavy favourite.

In hold'em you don't necessarily want to make the best possible hand. You want to make a hand with the best possible chance of winning – and in many circumstances that means a big pair with an ace kicker, rather than aces with a weaker side card.

This concept comes up quite often with straight and flushes. Suppose you're holding 8♥7♥ on the button with seven active players in an unraised pot. You call and miraculously flop the nut (unbeatable) straight when you see 6♥9♣10♥ hit the board. Not only have you flopped the nut straight, you also have a draw to a flush. Even a straight flush is a possibility, though it's a long shot.

You'd be happy seeing a couple of blanks on the turn and river. Anyone else who might have flopped a flush draw will pay you off until the river, and you can expect action from anyone holding J-10, A-10, overpairs, a set or two pair. But if a flush were to come and someone bet, you'd be on the defensive. Sure, a flush beats a straight, but in relative terms your hand just decreased in value – going from the nuts to the fifth-best flush. Now you won't be able to raise, and any call you make will be with a certain amount of trepidation. Unless you get very lucky and catch the 9♥ for a straight flush, you're going to be on the defensive for the remainder of the hand.

If you look around, you'll find numerous other examples of counter-intuitive strategies in hold'em. Just keep your eyes open to the possibilities and take advantage of them when you can.

Tip 33

Take Note of Note Taking

Keeping tabs on your opponents' playing styles by taking notes as you observe them is easily done online. To some degree this helps compensate for the difficulties in observing online opponents compared to the relative ease of observing an opponent's behaviour in a traditional brick and mortar casino.

Although it's easy to watch your adversary in a live game, it's tough to take notes on them. Some players bring notebooks into card games so they can take notes, but they're in the minority. Instead, players rely on their memory, or make notes on opponents after they step away from the table or when they get home.

Every leading online poker site provides screens for note-taking. You can take notes at your leisure, and a flag of sorts attaches itself to the player's screen name or avatar. Whenever your opponent enters the game, that flag is a reminder of notes taken about his play and you can review these observations with a click of your mouse.

Poker is a game of incomplete information, and the more information you have about a game and its players, the better decisions you can make. So take heed, and take notes. If you're unable to take notes on opponents unless you are playing in the game – most sites now allow you to take notes on players whether you're seated at that table or not – you can always use a word processor or a spreadsheet and then transfer the notes by copying and pasting once you've been seated in the game.

While observing, jot down playing styles, good and bad plays, betting patterns, behavioural patters, timing tells – such as unusually long delays when betting very good hands or an opponent's use of check boxes to fold poor hands instantly and raise with strong ones – and anything else that might give you a clue as to your opponents' hands.

Take note of who calls too frequently, as well as which players show the discipline required to fold a hand they might have raised with if it looks like they are beaten. Make note of check-raisers, outrageous bluffers and tight players too. List the stakes each player prefers so you can tell when they are playing below or above their comfort zone.

Taking notes is one of the most valuable features offered to online players and one of the easiest to use. Start taking notes the very first time you play online. If you begin in a play-money game, you'll be under no pressure and can master this valuable software tool as well as many others before you play for cash.

In most cases, you direct the note-taking function either by right-clicking above a player's icon or clicking a clearly designated button. A screen will pop up for you to type into. Although the note-taking procedures vary from site to site, all you usually have to do in most cases is rest your cursor over a player's seat to bring up any observations you've recorded. Some sites require you to click over a player's name or icon to reveal your notes.

You'd be surprised how many players ignore this feature. In fact, any time you become aware of someone who is playing in three or more games at once, you can be certain he's very unlikely to be taking notes too. Basic A-B-C, straightforward poker is the hallmark of a multi-table player. He really has no chance to take notes or pay close attention to games in progress when he has to make decisions at three, four, or sometimes as many as eight tables simultaneously. You can take advantage of your multi-tabling opponent's transparent playing style and limited decision-making time to trap him, bluff him and capitalize on the handicaps he's imposed upon himself.

Give top priority to note taking so that your notes will be available when you need them most – days or weeks later, when you encounter the same players again. Your notes will be automatically saved for you, but remember, the note-taking function can and probably will vary from site to site, so take nothing for granted. When in doubt, ask customer support or, if available, live help.

Tip 34

Playing Multiple Games Online

Playing a number of poker games online, which is called multi-tabling by adherents, is a fairly commonplace activity with experienced online players. It's also common among poker players who grew up as avid video-game players and became adept at zapping aliens, monsters or enemy soldiers coming at them fast and furiously from all directions.

Although online poker delivers far more hands than you can expect in a traditional casino – 100 hands per hour or more are common, compared to about 35 hold'em hands per hour in a brick and mortar cardroom – it doesn't provide enough action for some players. Giant screens and the ability to connect two monitors in tandem have made playing at two, four and even eight tables simultaneously more and more common among online players.

There are plusses and minuses to sort out if you're considering multi-tabling as a fact of online poker life.

First the bad news
You won't be able to concentrate on two games as well as you can on one, nor will you be able to focus on four or more games as well as you can focus on two. Everyone, it seems, has his or her own limit, and when this limit is exceeded, his or her concentration drops like a stone in water.

I've played as many as four games simultaneously, but three seems to be my limit. Yet I know of players who regularly log five hours or more per day playing up to eight tables simultaneously. Some multi-tablers claim to be able to play different games at different tables, which means shifting gears between hold'em and Omaha/8 – or whatever else you might be playing – which just adds to the potential confusion.

While I can see playing Omaha and hold'em simultaneously, I can't see how anyone can play seven-card stud and seven-stud/8 or Omaha high and Omaha/8 at the same time. The games look the same and it's too easy to get caught up in thinking about making a low hand in a game where low doesn't count.

It's also impossible to play a multitude of games while keeping up with note taking, so information about your opponents' playing proclivities is lost in the process. The bottom line is that you won't play as well in multiple games as you will when you focus all your mental efforts on one game.

Now the news you want to hear

Poker is not necessarily about playing well so much as it is about playing well enough to make the most money. And when you're playing at a couple of tables, you figure to make more money than you will at one table as long as you play better than your opponents. Let's assume that you can play at four tables, but you're only 75 per cent as effective as you are at one table. If you are able to win at the rate of two bets every hundred hands at one table, but win an average of 1.25 big bets per 100 hands on each of four tables, you figure to win five big bets in the hour it takes to play 100 hands at each of four tables. Even if you are only able to play two tables at once with any degree of skill and comfort, you are still ahead because you can squeeze out an average profit of 2.5 big bets per hour by playing two tables at once, whereas you'd only figure to win two big bets if all you played was one table.

If you can play two tables simultaneously, you can also play for smaller stakes, thereby putting less money at risk. If you play well, you should win just as much money but decrease the variance and fluctuations you experience in the process.

Tip 35

Fit or Fold

If you don't realize the importance of it by now, we'll emphasize it again: the flop is the defining moment in hold'em. You get to see 71 per cent of all your cards on the flop. That's right. For the cost of one measly bet before the flop, you can see five-sevenths of your entire hand. It's one of poker's biggest bargains.

But because of that, it's imperative that the flop fit your hand in order to warrant the relatively pricy decisions to see the turn and the river. Deciding to see the turn or the river means seeing fewer cards at an escalated price, and before you make this decision, you need to have something worth sticking with.

Fit or fold means a couple of things. The first and most obvious example of fitting or folding is that the flop should help your hand. If you begin with Q-J and the flop is Q-J-3 you've made two pair and were obviously helped by the flop. In fact, you could say it fit your hand like a glove.

If you began with a weak hand such as 4-4 in the big blind and flopped a set of fours, the flop smiled on you in an even bigger way.

But that's not the only way the flop can fit your hand. If you began with 9-8 and the flop was T-7-3 you flopped four to a straight and will probably get the right price from the pot to justify playing on in hopes of completing your straight draw. The same is true if you began with two suited cards and were fortunate enough to find two more of your suit on the flop. Now you have a four flush and that's usually a draw worth playing.

In addition to a flop that fits you because it paired your hand or provided a draw to a big hand, there's another way the flop can help you: by not helping your opponents at all. Suppose you begin a hand with a pair of queens and raise before the flop. You're rooting for a third queen on the flop, but there are a lot of cards you're rooting against too.

Even though you were the raiser before the flop, you still want to dodge a king or an ace, because those cards can give an opponent a pair higher than your queens. You'd also like to duck two or three mid-range or big adjacent cards because they increase the possibility of someone making two pair, a straight draw, or what's worse, a straight. If the cards are two-suited you have to fear a flush draw, and if they are all one suit another player might already have a flush.

But if the flop is J-7-3 of mixed suites it effectively fits your hand because it probably missed your opponents' hands. Unless someone has flopped a set – and the odds are against that – your hand, which was almost surely the best one before the flop, is probably still in the lead with only two cards to come.

This leaves you in good shape. You can bet and force any opponent with a lesser hand to take the worst of it if he or she decides to call. With the best hand, betting gets more money into the pot, and that's a good thing too. You are building a pot you are favoured to win, while making it more costly for any opponent to stick around in hopes of outdrawing you.

When you're playing Texas hold'em, here are a few general rules for playing the flop:

✓ Play if the flop improves your hand right now.

✓ Play if the flop provides a draw to a straight or a flush that figures to win the pot if you complete it.

✓ Play if you have the best hand before the flop and the flop is so ragged in texture that it figures to miss your opponents' hands as well as your own.

If none of these conditions are present, you can consider the flop to have missed your hand, and you have no reason to be in the pot – unless you have a valid reason to believe your opponent is likely to fold to a bluff.

Tip 36

Playing a Draw

Flopping a four-flush or an open-ended straight draw is a common situation. If it's relatively inexpensive, you'll invariably stay for the turn card – particularly when you're certain yours will be the best hand if you make it.

If you've flopped an open-ended straight draw, eight of the remaining 47 cards will help you.

But flush and straight draws are not the only drawing hands people play. If you have two overcards, six cards will pair you. If the board has paired one of your cards but it's not top pair, you're generally drawing to three-of-a-kind or you're hoping that you can pair your kicker to make two pair. When that's the case, five cards will help you. Four cards will complete an inside straight draw. Three cards will pair you if you have one overcard and think that you need top pair to win the hand. If you have a pair in your hand that's lower than top pair, only two cards in the deck will promote it to a set.

This is summarized in the following chart:

Common Draws

		Flop to River		Turn to River	
Outs	Type of Draw	Per cent	Odds	Per cent	Odds
9	Flush	35.0	1.86-to-1	19.6	4.11-to-1
8	Straight	31.5	2.17-to-1	17.4	4.75-to-1
6	Overcards	24.1	3.15-to-1	13.0	6.67-to-1
5	Pair	20.3	3.93-to-1	10.9	8.20-to-1
4	Two Pair	16.5	5.06-to-1	8.7	10.50-to-1
3	Overcard	12.5	7.00-to-1	6.5	14.33-to-1
2	Underpair	8.4	10.90-to-1	4.3	22.00-to-1

With a flush draw you've got a 35 per cent chance of completing your hand on the turn or the river combined, but if you miss on the turn, you have only a 19.6 per cent chance with the last card.

Expressed in odds, you're a 1.86-to-1 underdog to make your flush on the turn and river combined, but the odds against you increase to 4.11-to-1 against you if you're figuring the odds with only the river card to come.

Although many players stay with any draw all the way to the river regardless of pot size or the number of opponents, there's a better way to go about it. Here's what to do. Estimate the current size of the pot as well as how many opponents will stick around and pay you off if you get lucky.

If the estimated pay off exceeds the odds against making your hand, then your draw will show a positive expectation in the long run. Here's how this works. If you had to call a $10 bet into an $80 pot, the pot odds are 8-to-1, and if you're chasing a flush on the turn, the odds against making your hand are only 4-to-1. Because the pot odds exceed the odds against making your hand, you have a positive expectation – many poker players refer to this as a positive *expected value* or E.V. – and it pays to make this draw. If you could replay this situation thousands of times you'd show a profit in the long run.

The process of estimating pot odds versus the odds against hitting your hand can be confounded by the possibility that you'll occasionally make your hand but lose. Suppose you're holding A-Q of hearts and the flop is 7♥-7♦-6♥. You've got a draw to the nut flush. But you may be up against a full house or a set that can improve to a full house. The presence of a pair on the board should be a warning to any flush or straight draws.

Although big flushes are usually winners – straights lose to flushes, and it's not uncommon to pair overcards and lose with them – even when you flop a flush you can lose. Suppose you started with 9♥-8♥ and three hearts appeared on the flop, giving you a flush and what is probably the best hand. If another heart appears on the turn or river, putting four hearts on the board, anyone who comes out betting – and especially anyone who actually raises your bet – is likely to hold a very big heart and steal the pot right out from under your very nose.

It's important to realize the difference between making your hand and making a hand that will win the pot. They are not necessarily one and the same.

One of hold'em's most frustrating moments occurs whenever you turn a straight or a flush and end up beaten. When it happens it will try your patience. If you feel a sense of frustration, the best thing you can do is get up and take a walk through the casino until you cool down. When big hands get beaten, lots of otherwise good players go on tilt and start throwing off a lot more money than that one annoying hand just cost them. If it's any consolation, take solace in the fact that your big hands will hold up most of the time.

Tip 37

Raising with a Draw

If you're playing against good, savvy opponents who are aware of your playing style, you can't play the same way all the time and expect to have much success. Against alert opponents, a static style allows them to get a fix on your hand and take advantage of predictable play.

When your opponents are able to do that, they can deftly step out of the way whenever you have a big hand, but they'll pound you with all the weaponry at their disposal when they realize that they are in the driver's seat.

If you call a bet on the flop when two suited cards fall, call another bet on the turn but come out betting when a third suited card appears on the river, it's fairly clear to any reasonably astute opponent that either you were drawing and made your hand or you have a weak hand and are using that third suited card to provide a cloak of legitimacy for a bluff.

Your opponent can now step out of the way if he has a hand that cannot beat a bluff. He can also call with a hand that can beat a bluff but not a flush, and he can raise with a hand that beats your flush.

Your game will improve by adding some deception to it. By occasionally betting flush draws as though they were legitimate betting hands, you can accomplish a number of objectives.

Your opponent might not suspect you made a flush because you bet out, or even raised before that third suited card appeared on the board. This may give him all the impetus he needs to call your bets on the turn and the river once you complete your hand.

He might even come out betting himself. Then you can raise, especially if your flush is the best possible hand on the turn.

You can be aggressive with a draw whenever you have the right price to overcome the odds against making your hand, whenever you are getting the right implied odds to do so, and whenever the odds against completing your hand are not as long as they seem.

If you have four or five opponents on the turn, you can bet your flush draw or you can raise if someone else has bet. With that many players you are getting the right price on new money coming into the pot to offset the odds against completing your hand on the turn.

If you're in a hand with a group of opponents who call too often, you'll be getting great implied odds, which are a guesstimate of sorts as to how large the pot will be on the river. The greater the implied odds, the more it pays to play aggressively. On the other hand, if you are confronting a group of tight, timid opponents, you can't count on them sticking around to pay you off if you get lucky. But against loose, passive players, you will always get those additional calls to make your bets and raises worthwhile.

You can also play aggressively when you have a lot of ways to improve your hand. If you have A♦-K♦ and the flop is 9♦-5♦-2♣, you'll make the best possible hand if the next card is any one of the nine remaining diamonds in the deck, excepting the two of diamonds. You'll also make the best hand if a diamond comes on the river and the board does not pair, thus eliminating the possibility that someone just made four-of-a-kind or a full house. You also stand a good chance of winning even if you fail to complete your flush but pair either your ace or king. That will give you top pair with the very best kicker, and an opponent will have to make at least two pair to beat you.

When you are in these kinds of situations you can play your draws aggressively. You have a number of ways to win and the pot is usually large enough to overcome the odds against completing your hand.

When the time and the odds are right, you can pep things up by putting some deception into your game by aggressively betting and raising with drawing hands.

Tip 38   Slowplaying

Slowplaying is the act of trapping players by checking or by making only token bets with very big hands so that you can build the pot. The goal is to lure opponents into the hand so they become committed to it, then spring your trap on a later betting round.

If you're playing hold'em and flop a full house, you certainly don't want to come out betting on the flop in a fixed-limit game. You have the best hand and you'd like to give your opponents a chance to make a little something, or deceive them into thinking they can bluff you off the pot because you played your hand as though it were weak.

Let them bet, then call the flop. When they bet on the turn, you check-raise them. In a no-limit game you'll probably do this whenever you have a hand that's good enough to take an opponent's entire stack. Whenever you stand a chance of doing this, poker becomes a game of implied odds. When you are fortunate enough to make one of those very rare but very special big, big hands, you don't want to frighten your customers away.

The same concept holds true in fixed-limit poker too. But the amount you can win on future betting rounds is limited because of the wagering structure, and it's not nearly what you can win playing big bet poker.

Slowplaying is an art. Unless you flop some sort of near-unbeatable hand such as four-of-a-kind or a straight flush, slowplaying hands to give your opponents time and the opportunity to catch up is a two-edged sword. Whenever you risk giving your opponent a free card in exchange for the chance to win more money on a subsequent betting round, some of the time that free card will come back and bite you, unless your own hand is a mortal lock.

When that happens, you're left sitting there saying to yourself, 'If I'd only bet, he wouldn't have called and I would have won that pot. But instead, I got greedy. Serves me right.'

Is it worth it? It depends on how much of an underdog your opponent is and how big your own hand is in relation to his. In an ideal world, you want to give him sufficient latitude to make the second best hand, but not the best one.

If you flop two pair and there are two suited cards on the board, it's a tough decision. In a limit game, your opponent will usually call your bet if he has a flush draw. If you decide to try for a check-raise, your opponent may not bet and you will have succeeded in giving him a free card.

But in no-limit hold'em, if you knew he was on a flush draw, you could bet enough to price your adversary out of the pot simply by making sure that the cost of his call would not be priced correctly to support a flush draw.

Here's how that works. We'll assume you have a flush draw and there's $20 in the pot. I bet $100, so you have to call $100 to win $120. These odds do not offset the 1.86-to-1 odds against completing your hand, so drawing for your flush in these circumstances is not a good idea, especially if you sense that I will fire another salvo – and probably a bigger one – if the turn card is a blank.

Slowplaying is one of those two-edged swords that has risk as well as reward associated with it. Unless you have such a big hand that an opponent can never beat it, giving a free card comes with an element of danger. That's why pot-limit and no-limit hold'em players routinely price their opponents out of drawing hands.

In fixed-limit it's a dicey decision as to whether you ought to come out betting or try for a check-raise. That's never an easy choice, and the best course of action is usually rooted in an understanding of your opponent's playing style and tendencies.

Tip 39

Don't Let Your Opponents Read You

When you watch poker on television, you see the pros do this all the time: someone makes a big bet and while waiting for his opponent to fold, call or raise, he goes into the deep freeze.

He stares down at the table at a 45 degree angle. He pulls his ball cap down on his head and puts on his sunglasses so his opponent cannot look into his eyes. Some take it further than that. Poker pro Phil Laak always wears a hooded sweatshirt to the table, and when he finds himself in that situation, he pulls his hood around his face so you can't see any of his features at all. He's not called the 'Unabomber' for nothing.

Laak is so charismatic that he has attracted a legion of wannabees who love wearing hoodies just so they can mimic his antics when facing a tough decision.

But you don't have to go to the extremes of Phil Laak – you're not playing on television and getting the face time that comes with it. There's really no need to go that far over the top to prevent your opponents from deciphering your hand by reading the emotions in your eyes and on your face.

There are two equally valid ways to prevent giving out information about your hand at the poker table.

The first, and by far the most common, is to give out no information at all. If you act late in the betting order, you shouldn't even look at your hole cards until it is your turn to act. After all, if you don't know the cards you're holding, your opponents won't be able to get a read on your hand no matter what they do.

Once you look at your cards, put them down on the table. Place a chip or card protector on top of the cards and leave them there. There's no need to go back to your hand again, it's too big a tell. You'll remember that you're holding two clubs when another club falls on the turn or the river and gives you a flush, but it's usually more confusing when you're trying to recollect whether a certain card completes your straight. Players tend to look back at their hand to see if they've made a straight. They generally don't do that with a flush.

I'm not a big fan of sunglasses at the poker table. I've never yet been able figure out my opponent's hand from the look in his eyes. But I do look at a player's neck and his hands – a trembling hand is usually an involuntary sign of a big hand – as well as the general energy level of his bearing and countenance, to get a read on what he might have.

One way to guard against giving your hand away is to withdraw inwardly as though you're a turtle going into his shell – like Phil Laak disappearing into his hoodie – every time you make a big bet and are waiting for your opponent to decide what to do.

Another way to disguise yourself at the table is to broadcast too much information. This is exactly the opposite of the turtle approach. You can fidget to your heart's content, babble incoherently if that pleases you, and go through whatever hand and facial gyrations you can muster, secure in the knowledge that any valid information you're inadvertently giving off will be hidden in all the disinformation you are broadcasting along with it.

It's like a baseball manager flashing signs to the batter and runner. For each signal that means something, he's going through a litany of signs and hand gestures that have absolutely no meaning at all. They're only there to provide information overload to the opposition trying to 'read' him.

There isn't a right or wrong way to do this, except to make sure you choose a technique that's consistent with your own personality. If you are calm by nature, going through a fidgeting routine won't be as easy, or as convincing, as trying to throw off no signals at all. But if you are a natural born wiggle-worm, you might find that sitting stone still is tougher than it looks. If that's the case, spreading the seeds of disinformation – rather than no information at all – might be your cup of tea.

Tip 40

Bet 'em If You Get 'em

Many poker players are so fond of making slick, tricky moves at the poker table that they overdo it, fool themselves, and lose money in the process. Somewhere, for each game and each mix of players, there's a theoretical optimal rate for tricky plays like bluffs and check-raises.

It's impossible to calculate this frequency with any degree of precision. It is always in flux, even at the same table and even among the same mix of opponents. While we can't point to an optimal degree of tricky play, we do know that it does not lie at either polar extreme.

If you never did anything deceptive, your opponents would characterize you as a very straightforward player who is easy to read. If you never bluffed, never tried for a check-raise, and never mixed any form of deception into your play, your opponents would bet when you checked and fold when you bet – unless they had a really powerful hand, in which case they would raise – and take your money in the process. It would be as though you were playing with your cards face up, while their cards were face down.

If you pulled tricky plays all the time, by always betting weak hands as a bluff and always checking strong ones in order to pull off a check-raise, your opponents would also be able to figure you out. Whenever you check, they'll check behind you, but they'll raise whenever you bet one of your weak hands.

It's clear to every good poker player that the optimum frequency for fancy plays resides somewhere to the left of never and the right of always. Nevertheless, most poker players lean too far towards the 'always' side of that scale. In other words, they bluff and try for check-raises too frequently.

Deception is designed to accomplish three objectives:

✓ It will protect your true intentions because your observant opponents will know that your checks do not always imply weakness, nor do your checks mean that you're planning to raise if they bet.

✓ You can win money when you do bluff because your opponents will not be certain whether you have the goods or not. Because of that, they'll occasionally fold a hand that would have grown into an ultimate winner.

✓ If you do check a good hand, your opponents won't be sure what you have and might cooperate with you by betting into your planned check-raise.

Because most players lean a bit too far in the direction of tricky play, give some consideration to playing most of your hands in a straightforward manner by checking weak hands and betting good ones. Don't succumb to the temptation to get caught up in what poker expert Mike Caro refers to as 'Fancy Play Syndrome'. It's a common disease among players who are fond of proving to themselves and others just how tricky they can be. Unfortunately, all too frequently they wind up shooting themselves in the foot.

Those few occasions when you do get tricky provide cover for the straightforward plays you make most of the time.

Because most of your opponents will play too many hands and call far too often with hands that don't warrant it, you are better off betting your good hands and eliciting a call from your opponents who are prone to do that anyway. After all, if you check, they may check weak hands behind you in hopes of seeing the next card at no cost, and unless you have a very powerful hand, you are usually better off not giving an opponent a free card.

You can adjust this strategy when necessary by checking instead of value betting against an opponent who likes to bluff when you check. You can give him all the rope he needs to hang himself by checking your good hands, allowing him to bluff, and corralling that extra bet or two by calling his bet or even raising.

If you have an opponent who is very timid and folds to most bets, try betting some hands for value that you would otherwise check, and collect those pots that he would have won if only he'd had the courage to call your last bet.

Tip 41

The Gap Between Betting and Calling

Calling a bet or a raise requires a much stronger hand than is needed to do the betting or raising in the first place.

This is true in cash games and even truer in tournament poker. In a cash game you can reach into your pocket and buy additional chips whenever you need to. But when you lose all your chips in a tournament, you're done, finished, and all your hopes for a big payday are dashed.

Tournament players, because of the danger of elimination, are more prone to fold hands they would call a bet or a raise with in a cash game. And during some stages of a tournament the gap is even wider than usual.

In the main event of the WSOP, right before players make the money, play becomes incredibly tight. No one wants to play their hearts out for a couple of days only to be eliminated one spot before reaching the pay ladder. As a result, players with big stacks can frequently bet and take the pot. So many players are just hanging on, waiting for one more player to be eliminated so that they make the money. Many of these players won't play without a very big hand.

Because a large number of the players receive the same payout whether they are the lowest finisher on the pay ladder or wind up 20 places above that slot, play loosens up dramatically once every player reaches the pay ladder. Short-stacked players are now ready to gamble in order to move up a few rungs.

Once players reach the money, the gap shrinks dramatically, only to slow down again right before the final table is determined. There's a reason for that too. But now it's not money; it's face time. No one wants to come all this way and miss their chance to be featured on TV at the World Series of Poker's final table. Play slows down once again, only to return to normality once the television quotient has been established. The gap – while still present – is narrower than it was before.

Regardless of whether you're playing in a tournament or a cash game, the gap has an accordion-like quality to it, expanding and contracting depending on circumstances, playing strategies, the nature of the risk and the rewards, and the playing styles of those at the table.

While no formula can show you how to handle this gap, it always helps to know something about your opponents. When someone bets or raises, you should have some idea about the cards he requires before taking that kind of action. Once you know the range of hands he needs to bet or raise, you'll know what you need to call or re-raise.

If your opponent will raise before the flop with any pair between A-A and 9-9, as well as with A-K, A-Q, A-J, K-Q and K-J, you certainly don't want to call with a hand like Q-J, since all of your opponent's raising hands are in the lead and favoured to win the pot.

You should also fold a hand like 8-8. Although a pair of eights leads any of the big overcards your opponent might play, he will flop a pair approximately one-third of the time. When he does, you are behind unless you flop a set – and the odds against that are 7.5-to-1. Your pair of eights is also losing to any pair your opponent would play for a raise.

While your pair of eights is a big underdog against a larger pair and a small favourite against two bigger cards – players call this situation a coin-flip – you figure to lose in the long run by continuing to take the worst of it.

Even if your raising standards are exactly the same as your opponent's, you still need to fold most of your hands whenever he raises first. When he raises, you should call only with hands in the upper realm of those he'd raise with, and re-raise with hands like A-A, K-K or Q-Q.

Your opponent's raise contained a message. He's telling you that his hand is bigger and stronger than usual, and if you intend to confront him, you'll need a hand that's bigger and better than the majority of hands he'd raise with.

Understanding the gap and being able to exploit it when the time is right will save money when you fold certain hands you'd ordinarily call with. You'll also earn more money whenever your opponent is likely to fold, as well as on those occasions when he raises with a hand which is not quite as good as the one you're playing.

Tip 42

Raising Gives You Two Ways to Win

The themes of selective and aggressive play weave their way through much of this book. In fact, every credible poker author advocates selective and aggressive poker as a hallmark of winning play.

Aggressively betting and raising is usually superior to passively checking and calling. One reason for this is that raising gives you two ways to win, while passive play supports only one.

Suppose you have 8-8 and raise before the flop. One player calls your raise and both blinds fold, but the flop of J-7-5 misses you completely. If your opponent checks, you should bet. Here's why. The flop figures to miss him too, and if he entered the pot with two big cards, the odds are against his hand containing a jack. Your pair of eights is probably in the lead at this point.

If he does have a jack, you are a big underdog. But if he doesn't have a jack, and doesn't have a pocket pair of nines or larger, you are in the lead and your bet is an offer to your opponent to fold his hand.

If your opponent came out betting, you still might want to raise. In a heads-up encounter, the flop figures to miss both of you. Your opponent might bet to drive you off the pot. But if you raise, you've put the ball back in his court and now he has to decide what to do.

If he checks the turn you'll stand a good chance of taking the pot with a bet. You might have the best hand; you might not. It doesn't matter. The trick is in the betting. You make it difficult and expensive for him to keep calling with what he suspects is now the worst hand, and by doing so you give yourself two ways to win. You can win by convincing your opponent to fold, or you can win by having the best hand – which is the only way to win if you tend to play passively.

By betting and raising you charge your opponent a price to look at another card or give him an opportunity to fold. And that's just what you want to do. Your hand is not strong enough to lure an opponent into calling. It's the kind of hand that should be happy to win the pot right now, and the way to do that is to get your adversaries to fold. But they won't fold if you play passively. You have to be aggressive to convince them that folding is their best or wisest choice.

Convincing them that you have the strongest hand requires your willingness to commit money to it. With a middling hand, the best way to do that is through aggressive play.

For the cost of a single bet or raise you have a unique opportunity that you can never have by checking and calling. You can win in either of two ways, and if a good chance of winning only costs one incremental betting unit, the price is usually a bargain.

Tip 43

Raising Can Define Your Hand

Raising accomplishes a variety of objectives for savvy players. A raise can bring more money into the pot, and it can help you steal a pot when you don't have much of a hand at all. A raise can also help to define your hand and provide information about how well your hand stacks up against the opposition.

When your opponent bets and you call, you don't find out much about the quality of his hand at all. All you know is that he either has a hand that was worth a bet or he doesn't have a hand at all and is bluffing. When all is said and done, that's not much to go on. But if your opponent bets and you raise, you've created a scenario where you can find out a little something about his or her hand.

If you raise and he calls, you can be sure he has at least a reasonably good hand or a draw. He might also have a really strong hand and have called in hopes that you will bet again on the next round, thus gradually building a big pot that he feels he will win.

If your opponent calls with a draw, he is hoping to catch a card that completes his hand on the next betting round. The texture of the community cards frequently lets you know whether or not you're up against a drawing hand.

If the flop contains three different suits, it's clear no one has a flush draw, and if the gaps between the cards are large, there's probably not a straight draw out there either.

When your opponent bets and then calls your raise, examining the texture of the community cards is one of the necessary steps towards narrowing down the range of possible hands he might have.

If you're playing no-limit or pot-limit and you suspect your opponent might have a straight draw or a flush draw, you can always make a big enough bet so that he will not have the correct odds to call. If he's playing logically, he'll fold his hand whenever the prize isn't worth the price.

But if you're playing fixed-limit hold'em, all you can do is bet the proscribed limit. That's usually not enough to make drawing for a flush or a straight a mistake. But sometimes your choices in life, and in poker too, are between the lesser of two evils, and failing to bet gives your opponent the dreaded free card. That allows him to improve his hand at no cost to himself. In essence, a free card offers your opponent infinite odds to complete his hand.

If he misses, he's done so at no cost. If he makes his hand, he will be the one charging you a price to look him up at the showdown. At least betting makes him pay to play, and that's all you can do.

There's lots of available information you can put to good use at the poker table. Some of it is free, while other information comes at the price of a bet or a raise designed to give your opponent an opportunity to fold his hand. Even when he doesn't fold, calling, raising or re-raising ought to give you the information you need to determine how your hand stacks up against his and what you have to do about it.

Tip 44

Another Reason to Raise

Raising is usually a better alternative than just calling. Some reasons for raising, such as getting more money into the pot when you think you have the best hand, are obvious. Others are subtler, and considerably less transparent.

One of those finespun reasons involves raising when you know you have the worst hand. And not because you're trying to bluff either. There are times to put more money into the pot even when you don't figure to win it.

If that seems counterintuitive, it is. But much of poker's wisdom flies in the face of everything that appears to be both conventional and intuitive.

Here's an example. Suppose you call before the flop and find yourself in a raised pot with five opponents. On the flop you estimate your chances of winning at 20 per cent if all your opponents remain in the pot with you. Everyone checks to the gal who raised before the flop, and she comes out betting.

It doesn't matter what your hand is. All we're concerned about are your chances of winning this confrontation. For the price of a bet you can call, and if all five players remain active, there'll be a total of 15 small bets in the pot – two small bets per player when it was raised before the flop, and one bet per player on the flop.

With a 20 per cent chance of winning, you have equity equal to three small bets (a pot of 15 small bets multiplied by your 20 per cent chance to win equals an equity of three small bets). But what if you were to raise and eliminate all but the original raiser – the gal who made it two bets to go before the flop?

If your raise eliminates all but one opponent, we'll assume your chances of winning the pot increase to 40 per cent. After all, the chances of the three players who folded to your raise amounted to something – and we'll assume that their aggregated chances amounted to 30 per cent.

Your own chances of winning, along with those of your one remaining opponent, both increased when the other players folded. We'll assume that her chance of winning increased to 60 per cent and yours improved to 40 per cent. The equity has changed too. There were 10 small bets before the flop, but when your opponent bet and you raised, you each contributed an additional two bets to the pot, which now amounts to 14 small bets.

Although you're still an underdog to win the pot, your equity is now 14 small bets x 40 per cent = 5.6.

Isn't that interesting? You voluntarily committed more money to a pot you still don't figure to win, but your fair share of that pot has almost doubled in the process.

It's not as counterintuitive as it first seemed. Your raise convinced three of your opponents to fold, reducing their chances of winning the pot from a collective 30 per cent to 0. Since someone wins every pot, that aggregate 30 per cent has to go somewhere, and it is shared by you and your opponent. You both increased your chances of winning, and while she's still favoured to win the pot, that's less important than the increased equity you gain when some of your opponents fold.

What matters most from your standpoint is that your chances of winning more than doubled, and if you could replay this same scenario over and over again your raise improves your fair share of the pot from 3 bets to 5.6 bets.

It won't work out the same in every situation. And because you'll only be able to estimate each player's chance of winning while the hand is in play, and you won't be able to tell how many players will be eliminated when you raise until after they each decide whether to fold or play their hand, this process is just an educated guess and nothing more.

Nevertheless, whenever a raise causes one or more opponents – each of whom has some chance of winning the pot – to fold, their potential equity in the pot is redistributed among the active players. And while you still may be an underdog after you've raised, you can improve your chances in the process.

Poker is not always about securing a hand that's favoured to win. Sometimes your actions will be predicated on losing less money in the long run. Raising in order to steal equity from your opponents' hands by inducing them to fold is a terrific way to accomplish that.

Tip 45

Check-raising

When players are just beginning to develop their hold'em skills, the very first move that captivates their imagination is check-raising. It feels so good, so slick and tricky, never mind the fact that it gets more money into a pot you figure to win. There's just something so appealing about check-raising that many players overuse it – to their own detriment. Here are some guidelines you can use when wondering whether to come out betting or try for a check-raise.

The first rule of check-raising

Save your check-raises for when you believe you'll have the best hand if you are called to compensate for those occasions when you don't have the best hand and find yourself facing a re-raise. The exception to this rule is if you believe check-raising will induce your opponent to fold a better hand. Unless you believe that you'll have the best hand most of the times you are called, you should refrain from check-raising.

The second rule of check-raising

Before you decide to try for a check-raise, you need to be fairly certain your opponent will bet if you check. It's no fun to check a big hand only to have your opponents check behind you, especially when you know they would have called – if only you had bet. What's worse is that a failed check-raise results in giving your opponents a free card that might beat you.

If your opponent would have folded to your bet, but instead took a free card and beat you with it, it's a catastrophe. By trying for a check-raise that didn't pan out, you paid a high price: the entire pot.

If you're uncertain about whether your hand will win if you're called, or you're not quite sure one of your opponents will bet if you check, you're far better off betting than trying for a check-raise.

Sometimes even aggressive opponents who have been betting the entire hand will slow down when a third suited card appears on board. Since they've been doing the betting and you've been calling, it's natural for them to assume you have a drawing hand. When that third suited card appears or an apparent straight is on board, many players – even aggressive ones – apply the brakes.

If you're going to try for a check-raise when it appears that a drawing hand has been completed – and a third suited card is probably the most common situation of this sort – you need an opponent who is aggressive enough to bet right into the teeth of that completed draw before you decide to try for a check-raise. It helps if your opponent thinks you do not have a drawing hand.

Here's how you might be able to create that level of deception. Suppose you're in early position with A-J of clubs. Someone raises. You call, and the flop is Q♦-7♣-4♣. If you bet and your opponent holds A-A, K-K, Q-Q or A-Q, you'll probably be raised, if not on the flop then on the turn. If you check when an innocuous third club falls on the turn, your opponent might assume you were either trying to steal the pot from early position, or betting a hand like second pair to find out how it stacks up against the competition.

If your opponent doesn't consider a flush among your possible holdings, he has set himself up for a check-raise. When you check-raise, he'll realize he's beaten, but most players will call one additional bet even if they ought to know better.

By check-raising successfully, you've also enabled yourself to bet future marginal hands on the flop and get a free card on the turn if the board is threatening. Your deceptive check-raise will help you win additional money from your opponents, and even get you an occasional free card.

This only works against astute players who expend the effort to put you on a hand and then see whether your cards confirm their supposition. When they're wrong, you can create added manoeuvrability for yourself in the process.

But when your opponents are absolute maniacs, compulsive callers, or just unobservant types who play their own cards and don't even consider what their opponents might have, don't bother trying to fake them out. They will do whatever suits them, regardless of any seeds of misinformation you might have scattered in their direction.

Tip 46

Betting Patterns, Part 1

Identifiable betting patterns are there for you to spot in most poker games, and this information can help you gain an edge on others in the game. Every top-notch poker player is aware of betting patterns and how to capitalize on the information they provide.

If you've never considered the implications of betting patterns, don't feel like you're all alone. Many other players are blind to them too. Information gleaned from studying betting patterns serves a number of purposes – from tracking the playing styles of your adversaries to tracking down some parts of your own game that might need improvement.

The most common pattern you'll find in a hold'em game is one your opponents do all the time. You probably do it yourself. It goes like this: call, bet, bet, check. That's simple, isn't it? You call the blinds before the flop, catch a hand you like – something like top pair with a good kicker – so you bet the flop and the turn too, but when you fail to improve to three-of-a-kind or two pair, you decide to check the river to save a bet just on the odd chance that your opponent has the better hand.

Becoming aware of this most common of betting patterns allows you to pick up a small leak in your game. You're leaving money on the table. Do you see it?

Most of the time the river card won't promote your opponent's hand to one that's better than yours, as long as you had the best hand going into the river. When it does, it's usually a third suited card portending a flush or a sequenced card that has 'straight' written all over it. If a third suited card jumps out of the deck on the river, feel free to check as long as your opponents act after you do. But if you have the luxury of acting last, go ahead and bet. You're likely to be safe, not sorry, if you do.

A player who is fortunate enough to catch his flush card on the river will bet when it's his turn to act. And if he had a bigger hand than yours before the river – suppose he flopped a set, or the top two pair – he'll do his check-raising on the turn, not the river.

What's the message in this bottle? Most times you have the best hand on the turn, you'll have the best hand on the river too, and you ought to bet it. Okay, okay, so you'll run into some nasty situations when you bet and are called – or even raised – and lose the pot. Don't worry about it. It's no big deal in the grand scheme of things, because you're far more likely to attract a crying call from a weaker hand than you are to induce a raise from someone holding a stronger one.

If you habitually check the river with a hand like top pair and a good kicker, you leave money on the table – and you're not doing much for your image either. But this is about as easy a fix as it is in anyone's poker game. Just bet the river. That's all there is to it. Change your betting pattern from call, bet, bet, check, to this one: call, bet, bet, bet. It'll do a world of good. See for yourself.

Suppose you're on the other side of this coin and you don't think you have the best hand on the river. What should you do then? Well, the fact that you know your opponent is going to check all but the very strongest of his holdings gives you a chance to either show down your hand in hopes that it might a winner, or even bluff if he is capable of folding a hand that fits his habitual call, bet, bet, check betting pattern.

That's not too shabby, is it? You can save a bet any time you have a weak hand that you hope will win in a showdown, and you can take the entire pot on those occasions when you are savvy enough to recognize the kind of player who will release a marginal hand to a bet on the river, even when his hand is actually strong enough to beat yours.

Tip 47

Betting Patterns, Part 2

Betting patterns is a rich topic that's worth a continued look, and we'll begin with another common one: call, check/call, check-raise, bet. This is the hallmark of a player with a good hand. Perhaps he's flopped a set or two pair, or even an ace or a king to his A-K. So he checks and calls a bet on the flop, then check-raises the turn in hopes of trapping one or more players for two bets.

Once he check-raises, he continues to drive the hand by betting the river. There's nothing unusual here. This is probably the most common betting pattern employed by players holding big hands. They quietly call the flop in hopes of getting in a check-raise on the turn, then they bet out on the river.

Here's how an awareness of this betting pattern can help you. When someone checks and calls the flop, then check-raises the turn, credit this player with a big hand that's probably better than yours. While you might find some extraordinarily creative players who will check-raise-bluff every now and then, it doesn't happen all that often in most games, and almost never in lower limit games. If you're the target of a check/call, check-raise betting pattern, go ahead and throw your hand away unless you've got an extremely strong hand or a draw to a better hand than your opponent is likely to be holding.

Many players are reluctant to throw away a hand to a check-raise. As a result of their stubborn nature, they lose a big bet on the turn and another on the river. And they needn't do this. After all, most of the times you are check-raised, your opponent has the better hand. And most of the times he exhibits this betting pattern you should do the smart thing and throw your hand away.

If you do, you will have saved two bets. And money saved is equal to money won. Even if you are a consistently winning player who averages one big bet in the plus column per hour, calling a check-raise when you strongly suspect you are beaten will take two hours of play to recoup. When Kenny Rogers was singing 'you gotta know when to fold'em', this was his message.

There are other betting patterns to be aware of too. If you see someone play the pattern bet or raise, then fold, you've got an opponent who is sufficiently disciplined to throw away a hand such as a pair of jacks whenever an overcard flops and there's some action. Or he's disciplined enough to get rid of Big Slick – A-K suited or off suit – when the flop is small cards and there's some action by other players before it is his turn to act.

Here's another pattern to look for: bet, bet, check, and either check, bet, call or raise on the river. This is the pattern of a player who takes a free card when the circumstances suit him, and if he does this enough, you can mark him as a tough, disciplined foe.

There's more to be said about betting patterns – much more, in fact. But for those of you who have not thought much about identifying and cataloguing betting patters, this should serve as food for thought. If you're already scrutinizing betting patterns whenever you play, this should reinforce some of your own ideas. If you keep watching those betting patterns unfold when you play poker, you're on the road to becoming a winner for life.

Tip 48

Don't Send Signals If They're Not Watching

While a lot of the moves made at the poker table provide information to other players, sometimes plays are made intentionally to provide disinformation to opponents. Betting a weak hand as if it's a strong one, or checking a strong hand in hopes of convincing someone that your hand is weak so that they will bet and you can raise, are both examples of giving disinformation.

It's not only betting patterns that are used to convey disinformation across the table. There are multitudes of false tells that savvy players give out in order to induce another player to bet or check, or otherwise do just what the cagey player wants them to do.

Sometimes we appear timid. On other occasions we bluff with outrageous hands in situations where a bluff stands precious little chance of succeeding. We don't do this to win the pot, we do this to convince others at the table that we are unrepentant maniacs. We hope they see us this way and continue to play us this way. Then we can spring a trap on a future betting round, or even a few hands later, and capture a big pot by our slick play.

But if someone is completely oblivious to our titbits of disinformation, and plays his cards without any regard for the hand you might be holding, there's little chance that these slick, advanced, tricky ploys will succeed. There are players who will flop top pair and continue to bet into a dangerous board and a gaggle of opponents, when they really should apply the breaks and consider what their adversaries might be holding.

But they don't. And when you see this at the table, you can categorize your opponent as someone who pays attention to his hand and his hand only. If you were to ask him after the hand's conclusion, 'What did you think I had?' you're likely to get a blank stare in return, if he even acknowledges you at all.

There's no need to be tricky where these guys are concerned. Tricky implies sending a signal to another player, but before you bother signalling that player, you have to be sure that his or her radio is turned on and there's an ear that's listening.

When they are not listening, your job is very simple. Play straightforward, boring poker. Don't try anything tricky. Just bet your good hands for their own intrinsic value and check your weak ones. If your opponent is too loose – and this tends to be the *modus operandi* for these kinds of players – you'll get paid off in the end and save bets when your hands are weaker.

If you are up against a player who doesn't listen and is too tight – you won't run into too many of them, though there are a few – you can bet your better hands for value, check your middle-of-the-pack hands, and bluff a little bit more than you normally would, especially if your opponent is giving off clues that he is not all that thrilled about his hand.

It's fun to play creatively and exciting to run players off better hands than the one you're holding. But to do that, you've got to be able to convince your opponent that you have a better hand than he does. If your opponent is the kind of player who just doesn't listen to the signals you're broadcasting, there's not a chance that he's going to pick up the message.

When that happens, your tricky plays are doomed to fail and will cost you money you needn't have lost if you had just played straightforward poker. Although straightforward poker is not as much fun as playing creative poker, there are times when it's called for – and if winning money is your goal, then good, solid, basic, boring poker is sometimes the way to go.

Tip 49

When to Bet and When to Check

Here's a tip that's so simple, so obvious, that you'd think everyone knows it. But they don't. It's so simple that once you learn and understand its implications, you can gain a bet and sometimes save a bet with regularity.

If you are first to act and have a hand that might be the best hand, but you're not sure about it, what's the best course of action?

Let's assume, just to make this exercise philosophically pure, that you have a 50-50 hand. It's even money to win, which also means it's even money to lose. What should you do?

If you're first to act, consider betting. If you bet, you're even money to be wagering with the best hand. But having the best hand is not the only way you can win. You'll also capture the pot if your opponent throws away his hand, which he might well do if he has a 50-50 hand – just like yours – but is convinced that your hand is better. If he does this only 10 per cent of the time you'll be ahead, because you figure to win with the best hand 50 per cent of the times the hands are shown down and you'll also win all of the hands when he folds.

The equity you gain from folding will take an even money situation – one in which you don't figure to win or lose money on in the long run – and turn it into a situation in which you will win money simply because of the equity you gain when your opponent folds.

Sometimes your opponent might raise. He might do this with a 50-50 hand just to try and steal the pot. He might be successful too, because when you have a middling hand and are raised, it usually makes good sense to fold unless you also have a draw to a bigger hand than your opponent is likely to hold.

Nevertheless, your opponent doesn't figure to raise with mediocre cards anywhere near as often as he will probably fold to your bet, so this play wins money in the long run against most steady opponents.

But if you're last to act, there's no need to bet if you think your opponent will call and you might do better by taking a free card. But when you get to the river, this concept really comes into play.

If you are last to act and have a middling hand, you are usually better off checking and showing it down unless you think one last bet on the river will force your opponent to fold a better hand. This, however, won't happen too often. It's more likely that your opponent will fold his lesser hands but call – and sometimes even raise – with hands that can beat you. If he has a lesser hand than you, betting won't win any additional money, because you will also win if you check. But if you bet and are called by a better hand, you'll lose an additional bet. If you are raised, you might not even call the raise and you'll never know what might have been.

The best way to avoid these 'heads I win, tails you lose' situations on the river is to check, unless you think your opponent will call with a losing hand. The best way to determine this is to know your opponent's playing style, and that's another good reason to keep studying other players' styles when you're not involved in a hand.

Tip 50
Differences Between Fixed-limit and No-limit Hold'em

No-limit and fixed-limit hold'em are different games altogether, and successful strategies in one can lead to failure in the other. And it's all due to the betting structures.

In fixed-limit hold'em it's very difficult to price an opponent out of a pot. If you have a pocket pair of aces and your opponent flops a flush draw, he will have the right price to pursue his draw. And in any event, in a fixed-limit game it's hard to find a player willing to fold a pocket pair of aces unless there's a gun to his head.

Giving a free card is the worst of all possible worlds, because a free card provides infinite odds for the drawing hand. In this situation, all you can do by betting is make it somewhat more costly for your opponent to pursue his draw. Nevertheless, it's still correct for your opponent to keep calling.

But in no-limit poker you can manipulate the price your opponent is getting to the point where pursuing his draw is incorrect. You can bet enough into the pot so that he is getting just about even money when he's really a 2-to-1 or 3-to-1 underdog to make his hand. When this is the case he has to fold because he will lose money in the long run by taking this proposition.

Because of this, no-limit is a game where successes are achieved by trapping – not drawing – and by getting an opponent to commit his entire stack to a good hand when you have a better one.

In fixed-limit hold'em, money is won by finding and repetitively exploiting small edges. If you recognize mistakes an opponent will make, such as playing weak starting cards, you can hammer him when you have the best of it. He will lose smallish sums of money each time he loses a pot to you, but over time those losses will slowly mount up.

In no-limit, your opponent can play weak starting hands precisely because he is looking for a situation where he can trap you for all your chips. Playing a pair of fives from early position is usually not a good idea in fixed-limit games because even when you flop a set of fives and win, your wins won't overcome the losses that accrue when the flop doesn't favour your hand and you have to fold to a bet. But in no-limit hold'em, you can play a pair of fives in hopes that when you do flop a set, you might be able to take most or all of an opponent's chips.

Another critical difference between no-limit and fixed-limit is fear of folding. If you are unwilling to fold hands like top pair with the best possible kicker, two pair, and even sets on occasion, you will lose money in the long run in no-limit poker. No-limit poker is not a game that's based on pushing small edges, it's a game of trying to capture all your opponent's chips in one fell swoop.

To do that, you have to foster the illusion that all your chips are at risk too, although in reality you're not going to risk them as often as your opponents will. And there's your edge – risk your entire stack a lot less frequently than others and win money as a result.

The down side of this is that you will find yourself folding on the flop much of the time when another player makes a big bet and you're not quite sure of where you stand.

In a limit game, you can call one more bet and see if your hand wins the pot. But in a no-limit game, a lot more than one betting unit will probably be at stake. Losing your entire stack is usually too great a price to pay when you have a dicey hand in a risky situation.

The message here is twofold. First, fixed-limit games and no-limit games are as different as night and day. Second, while it often pays to call one last bet in a fixed-limit game, in a no-limit game, when your entire stack can be at risk on this betting round or the next one, discretion is often the better part of valour.

And as for those hybrid games – no-limit with a capped buy-in – they're sort of in-between. They play much more like a spread-limit game than either a fixed-limit game or a true no-limit game with its deep stacks that are always at risk.

Tip 51

Looking for Tells

Tells are nothing more than words, body language or other involuntary clues to a player's hand. When used in conjunction with an awareness of player betting patterns, they offer a powerful tool that provides information about an opponent's hand.

Tells are too powerful to ignore. Some are obvious; others are subtle. Some tells can be used with absolute certainty, while others may be accurate only part of the time. Moreover, a tell for one person might not be valid for another. Every tell has to be specifically interpreted for each player. The same physical manifestation that indicates a strong hand for John might mean a weak hand for Mary.

Tell Number One is the most common tell of them all, and it's simple: players holding weak hands act strong, and when they have a strong hand they act weak. You can rely on this tell with a high degree of certainty in most low-limit games, because the players aren't all that sophisticated – and they're not going to win an award for their acting ability. But it's not foolproof, because you'll always find some players who act strong when they are strong and weak when they are weak. But even when this tell is accurate only 70 per cent of the time, it's still a significant improvement over a guess, where your chances are only 50–50.

If you run across an extremely tough player who suspects you're a student of tells, he might throw a counter-tell your way just to confuse you. If he's sharp, he'll act weak when he's strong, and once he knows that you have a read on that, he'll reverse himself – but only with you. Now he'll act strong when he is strong. He knows you've read him for a weak hand, and he knows that you think he is attempting to win the pot by bluffing. When he knows that his counter tells have confused you, he'll probably start randomly interspersing counter tells with his normal style of play, so you'll seldom be able to read him accurately.

While any thinking player owes it to himself to be continuously alert at the poker table, it's safe to say that most of us are not reading tells as well as we could. It is nearly impossible to engage in the highly formative process of picking up tells, relating them to an opponent's playing style then taking advantage of them – all in the heat of battle. Because none of us will ever know all there is to know about tells, it would substantially benefit most players to spend their free time at the table looking for tells and observing other player's betting patterns.

When combined with observations about an opponent's betting pattern, an awareness of the cards that have been exposed, and knowledge of whether his playing style is tight or loose, or aggressive or passive, there is quite a bit of information available to assist each of us in making correct decisions.

Tells and other information picked up in the course of a game gives us the ability to divert from the *book play* in order to make a better play. In fact, the next time you see a top-notch player make what you consider to be an ill-advised play, you might just give him the credit he probably deserves. He may have been privy to information that was available to all – but only he was able to decipher it.

Tip 52

Looking for Tells in Cyberspace

When you play poker online, you don't have the same kind of tells available to you that you do when you sit across the table from live opponents in a brick-and-mortar casino. After all, when playing online, you have no idea about any physical manifestations your opponents might divulge in the heat of battle.

You can't read body language you can't see. You can't even tell if they are male or female, young or old, or seem experienced or not. But you do have some things going for you.

One way players reveal their hands online is through timing tells. This refers to the delay time between someone's opportunity to act and how long it actually takes that player to check or bet, or fold, call, or raise. Although most players fall into habitual patterns, these patterns differ for each player. As with visual tells that you'll pick up in a live casino game, each online tell has to be interpreted specifically for each player.

Thankfully, that's easily done online. When you're not involved in a hand, you should take notes on others at the table. In addition to noting the kinds of hands players turn up at the showdown, and the number of bets and raises they deemed worthy of the hand they played, you should note how long it took them to take each action they performed.

Many players use the action check boxes to fold, call or raise hands that don't require any kind of involved decision. When these players take a while to decide what to do, you should read them for a hand that's on the cusp of a decision. They don't know whether to fold or call, call or raise, or check or bet. If that's the case, and you've got a hand that doesn't leave you in a 'what should I do?' quandary, you can toss away marginal hands and raise with most of your better ones.

Other players are aware of the timing phenomenon and always delay acting when they have a very good hand in order to deceive their opponents into believing they have a marginal hand and are mulling over a tough decision. When this kind of player delays an inordinately long time before taking action and then raises, you can be sure he has a very strong hand and is trying to deceive you about its strength.

You'll only know for sure by studying players and taking notes about their play. Any time you run into the same opponent, even if it has been weeks or months and you don't recognize that player's screen name from the man in the moon, you'll have a set of notes on his playing style. Adjusting to his proclivities won't take you any more time than it does to read your notes.

Some players always play two, three or even four or more games simultaneously. Others do this occasionally, but not always. If your opponent takes a long time to make most decisions, you can use the game's software to locate him. If you find that he is playing in a couple of games at once, then his delay is not due to some sort of trickery, it's a function of his need to make a decision at another table before reacting to his options at this one.

These players generally play A-B-C poker. They are playing very basic strategies and don't have the wherewithal to be all that discerning of each table's texture, nor are they able to take notes on their opponents. They tend to bet their good hands, fold their poor ones, and play as straightforwardly as possible.

This is your opportunity to cast some seeds of deception in the direction of someone who is probably too involved in too many games for his own good. He is prone to folding when raised, because he needs to make decisions at other tables too. If you can keep him occupied with tough decisions, he might just decide that discretion is the better part of valour and fold in the face of your aggressive play.

Where Do You Go from Here?

While there are only 52 cards in a deck, we've added a 53rd tip. Consider it a wild card – a joker in the deck. It's not a tip per se, but a way of pointing you in the right direction if you're interested in increasing your poker knowledge.

Today's hold'em players have a variety of tools available to assist in raising their game, from books and videos to computer software that allows you to play the game while getting advice as you practice. You can also access any number of Internet chat forums or hire a personal poker coach.

Poker is a subtle game, full of nuances and strategic ploys that take some time to learn and apply in the heat of battle. But poker is not arcane, and it's not difficult. Anyone who wishes to improve his or her game can do so by accessing any or all of these learning tools.

There have never been more poker tools available than there are right now. If you take anything at all from this book, take this: keep learning and keep improving. If you do, you're very likely to improve more rapidly than other players. And when that happens, you'll wind up as the best player in the game. That's nice, isn't it?

Glossary

all-in (adv) To be out of chips after putting the remainder of your chips into the current pot when others still have chips and can continue betting.

all-in bet (n phrase) A bet made by a player that commits all his chips to the pot.

ante (n) One or more chips put into each pot by each player prior to the cards being dealt.

banana (n) A term usually heard in 7-stud/8. It refers to high cards that don't help a player who is drawing to a low hand. 'I started with 5-4-2, caught an ace on fourth street, then nothing but bananas all the way to the river!'

bet (v) A wager. 'I bet,' said Joe, as he placed his wager in front of him.

betting round (n phrase) The sequence of play during which each active player has the option, in turn, of folding, betting or raising, in order to address previous checks, bets or raises by folding, calling or raising.

bicycle (n) In lowball, the best hand, which is 5-4-3-2-A. In high poker, a bicycle, which is also called a 'wheel', is a 5-high straight.

blind (n) A mandatory bet made by a player before he gets his cards. It is part of that player's bet, as opposed to an ante which is part of the pot.

bluff (v) A bet made to represent a strong hand by a player with a weak hand who is attempting to convince his opponents to fold their hands.

board (n) In hold'em, Omaha, Omaha/8, Pineapple and Crazy Pineapple the board is the term used to describe the communal cards that all players use in conjunction with their personal cards to form the best poker hand or hands. In seven stud, 'board' refers to a player's exposed 'upcards'.

book play (n) refers to 'playing by the book', or playing a hand the way it is supposed to be played according to 'conventional wisdom'.

brick (n) A card that does not help your hand. 'I flopped a four flush, but the turn and river cards were both bricks.'

bring-in (n phrase) A mandatory, token, opening bet on the first round of play in a stud game that's usually an amount lower than the normal betting limits for the game. In a $20–$40 7-card stud game, the antes are typically $3 and the bring-in is usually $5. The player to the left of the bring-in can fold, call the $5 bring-in bet or complete the bet to $20 – which constitutes a full bet.

button (n) A small puck indicating the dealer position in games dealt by a house dealer. The term also refers to the player in that position. 'I opened the pot but the button raised.'

call (v) To match someone's wager.

check (v) A check is a bet of nothing. A player can check and retain his option to fold, call or raise any bets made by players acting after he does in the betting order. A check (n) is also a synonym for a chip.

check-raise (v) To check a good hand, and then raise when someone bets and the action returns to you. Also referred to as **sandbagging** or **slowplaying**.

chip (n) A small disk about the size of a silver dollar used instead of cash, with different colours used to represent various monetary units.

cold-call (v) to call a bet and one or more raises without having yet committed any money to the pot. 'Joe bet, Tommy raised, but Dave cold-called two bets.'

community cards (n phrase) In hold'em and other flop games, community – or communal – cards are those dealt to the centre of the table and are part of each player's hand.

connectors (n) Two sequenced starting hold'em hole cards, such as T-9 or 7-6.

counterfeited (adv) Having a card in your hand duplicated by a communal card on the board, thereby weakening your hand. In Omaha/8, you hold 8-6-2-A and the board is 8-7-3, giving you the best possible low hand of (8-7-3-2-A). If an ace or a deuce appears on the turn or river, you have been 'counterfeited' because another player at the table can now make a better low hand than yours.

crying call (n phrase) Reluctantly calling, and usually whining that you are beaten before even looking at your opponent's hand at the showdown.

cutoff seat (n phrase) The seat to the right of the player with the dealer button. The cut-off is next to last to act in the betting order.

dangler (n) In Omaha, a card that doesn't relate to the other three starting cards. For example, a starting Omaha/8 hand of 9-4-2-A contains three cards that work together and one that does not, the nine. That nine is said to be a 'dangler'. It does not work in concert with the other three cards because it cannot be used for low and will only make a high hand if at least two more nines appear on the board.

dealer button (n phrase) synonymous with 'button'.

deuce (n) A card with the rank of 'two'. By extension, any 'two', such as a two-dollar bet, a $200 bet or a $2,000 bet, can be made by saying 'I bet a deuce'.

door card (n phrase) The first exposed card of a hand in a stud game.

down card (n phrase) In a stud game, the hole cards that are not exposed for others to see.

draw (n) In Draw Poker, it refers to the exchange of cards players choose to discard and their receipt of new cards to replace them. 'Draw' also refers to an attempt to make a particular hand, such as a flush draw or straight draw. A player with two hearts in his hand who sees two more hearts on the flop in a hold'em game is said to be 'on a flush draw', because he needs one more heart on the turn or the river to complete his hand.

drawing dead (v phrase) A draw to a hand that will lose even if completed. If a player is drawing to a flush when an opponent already has a full house, the player on the draw is said to be 'drawing dead'.

draw out (v phrase) To catch a card that propels you to victory. 'I knew Tom had a straight, but I've had four hearts and was hoping to draw out on him.'

expectation (n) 1. The average profit or loss of a bet over a period of time. If I am a 2-to-1 underdog, but the pot will be five times the bet I must call if I win, I have a positive expectation. If I am required to call a $10 bet in order to win $50, I will win that bet one time in three in the long run. If this situation was to be repeated 99 times, I figure to win $50 on 33 occasions, an equivalent of $1,650 (50 x 33). But I figure to lose ten dollars 66 times, for a loss of $660 (10 x 66). My net win will be the difference between $1,650 and $660, or $990. Over the course of 99 hands, my expectation is $990 divided by 99 hands or ten dollars per hand. Thus my 'expectation' is positive, whether I win this particular confrontation or not.

expected value (n phrase) Expectation expressed as a dollar amount. In the example above, the 'expected value' is ten dollars. 'Expected value' is often referred to as 'EV'.

family pot (n phrase) A pot with a lot of players active in it.

fit the flop (v phrase) A hand is said to 'fit the flop' when it is helped by it. A hand such as J-T will fit the flop if the community cards are J-T-4, J-4-2 or 9-8-7.

fit or fold (v phrase) The idea that folding is the best course of action unless the flop helps one's hand by making a pair, two-pair, a set or provides a draw to a big hand such as a straight or flush. If the flop misses one's hand completely, unless the starting hand was strong to begin with, it usually makes better sense to fold than to continue contesting the pot.

fixed-limit (n phrase) As compared to pot-limit or no-limit, fixed-limit poker is a betting structure in which all bets are made in specified increments, such as two dollars and four dollars, usually referred to as $2–$4 limit.

flop (n) In hold'em and Omaha games, the three community cards turned face up after the first round of betting. The term 'flop' is also used as a verb, such as 'I flopped two pair'.

free card (n phrase) A situation where everyone checks on a given betting round and each player gets to see an additional card without the necessity of risking more money.

full of (adj phrase) The composition of a full house, described by stating the three-of-a-kind component first, followed by the pair. Thus the hand 4-4-4-9-9 will be described as 'fours full of nines', sometimes shortened to 'fours-full'.

gut shot (n phrase) An inside straight or a straight draw that can be filled by only one of four cards, not one of eight, as is common with an outside straight draw. A draw to 5-6-8-9 is a gut shot straight draw that can only be completed by catching a seven.

hand reading (adv phrase) The art and skill of determining the hand – or possible hands – an opponent might have through a combination of his betting patterns and the community cards on the board. An obvious example is a player who checks and calls in a hold'em game until a third suited card appears on the river. When he comes out betting, it's usually a case of a player whose flush draw has just materialized.

heads-up (adv phrase) Two players contesting a pot are said to be playing 'heads-up'. When a tournament is down to only two contestants, the tournament is said to be 'heads-up'.

hitting the flop (v phrase) To be helped by the flop, usually in a significant manner. 'Joe was hitting the flop with regularity; every hand he played caught the flop in a big way.'

hole card (n phrase) A card that has been dealt face-down to a player in a stud or hold'em game.

implied odds (n phrase) The ratio of what you think you will win, including money likely to be bet in subsequent rounds, compared to the cost of a bet. Because it includes speculation about money to be won on subsequent betting rounds, implied odds are more an estimate than a precise calculation.

kicker (n) The unpaired side card accompanying a player's pair or three of a kind. In hold'em, the rank of the kicker often determines the pot's winner. A-K will win by virtue of kicker strength against A-Q if the board is A-J-6-5-2, because A-K-J-6-5 is better than A-Q-J-6-5.

miracle card (n phrase) A long shot card that completes a player's hand. 'All I had was a miserable pair of deuces until I caught that third deuce on the river and beat Kathy's pair of aces. That third deuce was a real miracle card.'

money favourite (n phrase) When you are favoured to win money in the long run because the size of the pot compares favourably with the size of the bet.

no-limit (n phrase) A betting structure in which a player may bet all of his chips, as opposed to a fixed-limit game or a pot-limit game which has wagering restrictions.

nut flush (n) The best possible flush at any point in a hand.

nut low draw (n phrase) in Omaha/8, or 7-stud/8, a draw to the best possible low hand. If the Omaha/8 board is J-7-2, then a player holding A-3-x-x will have 7-3-2-A as a draw to the nut, or best possible low hand.

nut (n) A hand that cannot be beaten in any given situation. If the board is Q-9-7-3-2 and three of those cards are clubs, then any player holding the ace of clubs with any other club will have the nut hand. But if the board were Q-9-7-3-3 the nuts would now be four treys, followed by queens full of treys, then nines full of treys, etc. Because the board itself is paired, an ace-high flush is no longer an unbeatable hand.

Omaha (n) A hold'em game requiring players to use exactly two of their four downcards in combination with three of the community cards, and is differentiated from Texas hold'em, in which both, one, and sometimes even none of a player's personal cards are used. Omaha usually features four downcards, but variations of Omaha games are played with five or even six downcards for each player.

Omaha/8 (n) A form of Omaha played as a high-low split game, in which players can win a portion of the pot with a low hand of eight or better and with a high hand. If there is no qualifying low hand, the high hand wins the pot. It is possible for one player to win both the high and low sides of the pot.

on a hand (n phrase) Usually used in conjunction with hand reading. 'When the ten came on the turn, and Joe came out betting, I figured he had a straight, but he plays so erratically that's it's tough to put him on a hand.'

playing zone (n phrase) That portion of a deck containing cards most likely to be favoured by players. In Texas hold'em, the high end of the deck is the playing zone, but in Omaha/8, because players are attempting to make low hands as well as high ones, playing zones are the high and low ends of the deck, with players generally eschewing mid-range cards such as T-9-8-7.

pocket pair (n phrase) Any pair dealt as one's first two cards in hold'em or as part of one's first three cards in stud games.

poker (n) Any of variety of card games played by two or more players who make one or more wagers on the value of their hands.

pot (n) Chips that have been wagered on a particular hand. Also the centre table area in which wagers are placed by the dealer. 'How much is in the pot?'

pot-limit (n phrase) A structure of poker wagering limits that is defined by the current size of the pot. A raise can include the size of the pot after a call is accounted for. If there is $50 in the pot and Roger makes a pot-sized bet of $50, Deirdre can raise the pot by first calling Roger's $50 bet, then raising $150, which is the amount in the pot after her call of Max's bet is accounted for.

pot odds (n phrase) The ratio of pot size to the size of a wager facing a player who wishes to continue in a pot. In a $100 pot, if you are facing a $20 bet, your pot odds are 5-to-1.

premium pair (n phrase) Generally used in 7-card stud games to describe a starting hand that contains a pair of tens or higher.

private cards (n phrase) Cards dealt to each player face down. In hold'em, it's your first two cards, in Omaha the first four cards are private and dealt face down (as compared to the communal cards that can be played by all active participants and are dealt face up) while in 7-card stud and 7-stud/8, private cards are the two down cards dealt as part of the first three cards, and the last card. These cards are 'private' in the sense that their identity is not known by anyone other than their holder.

put someone on a hand (v phrase) to figure out a player's hand from a combination of betting patterns, exposed cards and physical tells.

qualifier (n) A certain hand or better, that a player must hold in a high-low split game in order to win half the pot. In most high-low split games, an eight low, that is, five unpaired cards with the rank of eight or lower, are needed for a player to make a low hand that is eligible to win half the pot. There is typically no qualifier required for a high hand.

quartered (adj) Winning one quarter of a pot by splitting the low half of the pot in an Omaha/8 game.

raise (v) To increase the bet after someone has made a wager before it is your turn to act.

re-raise (v) To increase the bet after someone has wagered and another player raised before it is your turn to act.

river (n) The fifth community card in Texas hold'em or Omaha, or the seventh card in a stud game. In any case, it refers to the last card dealt in a poker game or the last round of wagering.

rolled up (adv phrase) Being dealt three of a kind as your first three cards in a stud game. 'Barbara was dealt rolled up eights; there was no way anyone could dislodge her from that hand.'

scare card (n phrase) An exposed card that looks to have improved a player's hand. A fourth exposed heart in a player's 7-card stud hand is a scare card because it makes a heart flush very likely. In Texas hold'em a flop of Q-J-T is scary because it portends a straight, two pair (because those cards are all in the playing zone), or even a flush or flush draw if three or two of the cards are suited.

scoop (v) To win the entire pot in a high-low split poker game by making both the highest and the lowest hand, or by having the winning high hand when no-one has a qualifying low hand.

semibluff (n) Betting on a hand that is not the best hand at the time the wager is made, but is a hand that can improve and win the pot on a subsequent round. Semibluffing is most common with a flush or a straight draw because the semibluffer can win if his opponents fold, and is likely win if his opponents do not fold but he completes his hand.

set (n) In hold'em or Omaha, three of a kind in which a pocket pair combines with another card of the same rank that's present in the community cards. A 'trip', by comparison is made when one of a player's private cards combines with a pair on the board.

seven-card stud, also written 7-card stud (n phrase) A form of poker characterized by each player being dealt two cards face down and one face up followed by a round of betting, then three cards dealt one at a time together with a round of betting following each card, and one final card dealt face down to each player along with a final round of wagering.

seven-stud/8, also written 7-stud/8 (n phrase) A version of 7-card stud in which the high hand splits the pot with a qualifying low hand composed of five distinct cards with the rank of eight or lower. If there is no qualifying low hand, the high hand wins the entire pot. Players may play for high, play for low, or make a low and a high hand that enables them to scoop the entire pot.

showdown (n) The point at which all the cards have been dealt and all the wagering is complete and each player turns his cards face up to determine the winning hand – or hands.

side pot (n phrase) A pot created when one or more players run out of chips and other players still in possession of chips continue wagering. An all-in player cannot win the side pot, but is eligible for the main pot. More than one side pot can be created, depending on when players are all-in during the play of a given hand.

slowplay (v) To refrain from raising with a powerful hand in order to trap opponents on a latter, and usually more expensive betting round in a fixed-limit game.

spread-limit (n phrase) A betting structure that combines features of fixed-limit and no-limit wagering, and ranges from a minimum to a maximum with a spread significantly larger than the typical fixed-limit structure in which the betting limits double on the turn in hold'em, Omaha, or which betting limits double on fifth street in 7-card stud. A typical spread-limit game is $2–$10 hold'em, in which bets and raises can be made in whole dollar increments between two and ten dollars at any time, with the proviso that any raise must be at least as large as the bet preceding it.

standard deviation (n phrase) A descriptive statistical measure of the square root of the variance. In poker it is used as a measure of the variance one experiences in a poker game.

street (n) The number of cards that have been dealt, expressed by a number. When your fifth card has been dealt in 7-card stud, betting limits are said 'to double on fifth street'. The term is used more frequently in stud games, where players talk of third street, fourth street, fifth street, etc. In hold'em and Omaha games, players refer to the betting rounds as before the flop, on the flop, the turn and the river.

string raise (n phrase) A raise that is not made in one motion. If a player commits money to the pot, does not announce that he is raising by saying, 'I raise', then goes back to his stack for more chips, any other active player can call 'string raise'. The offending player may then only call the preceding bet, or wager as many chips as were in his hand before he reached back to his stacks for more chips.

tell (n) A verbal, physical or other mannerism that gives your opponents a clue to the strength of your hand. Tells can be inadvertent, such as a trembling hand indicative of a strong holding, or a false tell, such as acting weak with a strong hand or vice-versa.

ten-point cards (n phrase) Any card with the rank of ten or higher. This expression is usually used by Omaha/8 players to refer to a playable high starting hand combination comprising four, ten-point cards. 'I had a pair of jacks along with an ace and a queen, so with a 40 point hand, I had to raise.'

Texas hold'em (n phrase) The most popular form of poker played today, which features two cards dealt face down to each player followed by a round of betting, then three community cards (called the flop) dealt face up followed by a round of betting, a fourth community card (the turn) followed by a round of betting, and a fifth and final community card (the river) followed by a final wagering round. Although the true name of the game is Texas hold'em, it is usually referred to as just hold'em.

toke (n) A tip given to the dealer, usually upon winning a pot.

top pair (n phrase) In hold'em or Omaha, when a player pairs one of his hole cards with the highest card on the board.

trey (n) A card with the rank of three.

trips (n) In hold'em or Omaha, three of a kind made when one of a player's private cards combines with a pair on the board. A 'set', by comparison, occurs when a pocket pair combines with another card of the same rank that's present in the community cards.

turn (n) the fourth communal card in hold'em. It is preceded by the flop and followed by the river. The term is also used as a verb, in which a player who completes his straight on the turn might say, 'I turned a straight'.

weak-tight (adj) A characteristic used to describe a player who is timid and plays few hands.

wheel (n) A term that derives from ace-to-five lowball in which the best hand possible hand is 5-4-3-2-A. It is also called a 'bicycle'. The term is used in other games too, although in a game like hold'em, 5-4-3-2-A might not be the best possible hand. In Omaha/8, a wheel will always be the best possible low hand, and may also qualify as the best possible high hand, enabling the holder to scoop the entire pot.

win rate (n phrase) The amount of money a poker players wins per standard unit of time played or hands dealt. It is analogous to a batting average in cricket. Joe said, 'My win rate is one-and-a-half big bets per hour', while Mike might say, 'I'm winning three big bets per hundred hands playing $10-$20 Omaha/8'.

wrap-around (n) When four Omaha downcards consist of three sequenced cards that combine with the flop enabling a large number of cards on the turn or river make a straight. If your downcards are 6-5-4-A, and the flop is 7-8-Q, you can make a straight with any 6, 5 or 4 (three of each rank remain) or any of four 9s. In this scenario, 13 cards will complete your straight.

Index

Acknowledgements

I was seven or eight years old when my dad taught me to play poker. One night a week he hosted a game with his cronies in our Brooklyn neighbourhood. After driving my mother crazy with my badgering, she finally relented and let me stay up way beyond my normal bedtime to watch the guys play poker. I discovered my element and I loved it. All the players helped explain the rules to me, and after a while it began to make sense.

I was given only two restrictions: never give away anyone's hand and never repeat some of the more colourful phrases I heard at the table in front of my mother. Most of the Yiddish and Sicilian epithets I know today, I learned as an eight-year-old kid watching a poker game at our kitchen table.

I didn't realize it at the time, but I was hooked – even though I never grew up intending to play poker and write about it. But the seeds were sewn and I want to thank my dad, who died way too young, for pointing me in this direction. I want to thank my mom too. She lived a long, full life and always trusted her sons to do the right thing, even when it came to all-night poker games, the insane deadlines writers learn to live with, or both.

I've met some of the most interesting people in my life through poker and all of them have been encouraging. Al Alvarez, author of *The Biggest Game in Town* and a major figure in contemporary literature, was kind enough to encourage me over dinner at the Victoria Club in London when I was immersed in my first book and filled with doubt. I'm sure he had no idea how helpful his advice was, but I'd like to thank him for his encouraging words. All of my books leave a trail that hark back to his kind words about my writing.

There are other poker writers I admire and they've all become friends as well as colleagues. This group includes: Dave Scharf, Amy Calistri, Barbara Connors, Pauly McGuire, Ashley Adams, David Apostolico, Matt Lessinger, Dr. Al Schoonmaker, Dr. Arthur

Reber, Max Shapiro, Barbara Enright, Anthony Holden and Kathy Watterson. I also want to thank Mickey Wilson at PokerMagazine.com for providing an online outlet for my writing, and Chuck Weinstock at ConJelCo, as well as Howard Schwartz and Maryann Guberman at the Gambler's Book Store for selling my books and providing a lot of encouragement to a lot of poker authors.

I would also like to thank everyone who attends BARGE, poker's annual gathering of players who form friendships online and continue them in person every year. You are surely poker's brightest and best.

Thanks also to the folks at Royal Vegas Poker for their continuing support and encouragement and to Ron and Amber Oberman, Paul and Kimyo Zibits, Linda Johnson, Jan Fisher, and Mark and Lisa Tenner. Thanks, too, to all the guys and gals at the home game in Orange County that I almost never attend since I moved to Palm Desert, but whom I see periodically anyway.

Thank you to long-time friends Dan and Sharon Goldman, Nolan and Marietta Dalla, and to the gang that plays online every Wednesday night in Royal Vegas Poker's 'Play the Experts' tournament: Max Shapiro, Barbara Enright, Dr. Al Schoonmaker, Mike Cappelletti, Matt Lessinger and Rose Richie.

Thanks to Wade Andrews and the gang over at www.holdemradio.com for taking a chance on *Keep Flopping Aces*, the internet radio show that Amy Calistri and I host, which broadcasts in real time, worldwide, every Thursday night at 9:00 PM Eastern Time, and can even be listened to as a podcast available from iTunes.

I also want to thank Rick and Barbara, Stan and Phyllis, Marv and Joyce, Mike and Marci, Lenny and Susan, Alan and Myrna, George and Fran, George and Rita, and a few others who have been my friends since elementary school and high school. All in all it's been a grand life.

Thanks to Tina Persaud and everyone else at Anova, though I know you only through email. You did a wonderful job in getting this book together.

I began these acknowledgments with family and I'll end with family too. Thanks to David, Karen and Abby, and to Philip, Quinn and Michael, and to Shannon and Shandie, and to Heather, Scott and Shelby too. Special thanks and acknowledgement to my wife, Deirdre Quinn, who managed to make her way from Sligo, Ireland to Montana, then Washington and finally to Palm Desert in California. It was there she learned that hot climates trump cold ones, and how to nurture a moderately compulsive writer, poker player and husband.

About the Author

Lou Krieger is the prolific author of eleven top-selling books on poker. In addition to *52 Great Poker Tips*, they include: *Hold'em Excellence: From Beginner to Winner; More Hold'em Excellence: A Winner for Life; Poker for Dummies; Gambling for Dummies; Internet Poker: How to Play and Beat Online Poker Games; Winning Omaha 8 Poker; The Poker Player's Bible; Secrets the Pros Won't Tell You About Winning Hold'em Poker; The Rules of Poker: Essentials For Every Game;* and *The Portable Poker Pro.*

Lou Krieger wrote a bi-weekly poker strategy column for *Card Player* magazine for more than a decade and currently writes a bi-weekly poker strategy column for *Poker Player* newspaper. In addition, he writes for *Inside Edge, World Player,* PokerMagazine.com, *Canadian Poker Player, Midwest Gaming and Travel,* and *Woman Poker Player.* He also hosts a poker radio show called *Keep Flopping Aces,* which can be heard live online at www.holdemradio.com every Thursday at 9pm (Eastern time zone, USA). The show can also be heard in archived form at holdemradio.com, as well as in podcast format in iTunes.

In 2000, Krieger was named one of the top 100 gaming writers of the past 100 years by *Casino Journal,* the industry bible. It was an honour accorded only five poker authors. When not writing about the game, Lou Krieger can usually be found playing poker in the casinos and cardrooms of southern California.